TERESA OF AVILA

TERESA OF AVILA: *Selections from* The Interior Castle. Original translation published by Paulist Press, 997 Macarthur Boulevard, Mahwah, NJ 07430; www.paulistpress.com. Copyright © 1979 by the Washington Province of Discalced Carmelites, Inc. Introduction © 2004 by Dallas Willard. Foreword © 2004 by Patricia Hampl. All rights reserved. Printed in the United States of America. No part of this book may be used or reproduced in any manner whatsoever without written permission except in the case of brief quotations embodied in critical articles and reviews. For information address HarperCollins Publishers, Inc., 10 East 53rd Street, New York, NY 10022.

HarperCollins books may be purchased for educational, business, or sales promotional use. For information please write: Special Markets Department, HarperCollins Publishers, Inc., 10 East 53rd Street, New York, NY 10022.

HarperCollins Web site: http://www.harpercollins.com
HarperCollins®, ☕®, and HarperSanFrancisco™ are trademarks of HarperCollins Publishers, Inc.

Book Design by Susan Rimerman

FIRST EDITION

Library of Congress Cataloging-in-Publication Data is available upon request.

ISBN 0–06–0576472
04 05 06 07 08 RRD(H) 10 9 8 7 6 5 4 3 2 1

TERESA OF AVILA

Selections from *The Interior Castle*

Foreword by Patricia Hampl

Introduction by Dallas Willard

Edited by Emilie Griffin

Translation by Kieran Kavanaugh, O.C.D.,

and Otilio Rodriguez, O.C.D.

HarperSanFrancisco
A Division of HarperCollinsPublishers

CONTENTS

FOREWORD

The chronicler of mystical experience labors at a distinct narrative disadvantage as a memoirist. After all, by definition spiritual transcendence resides beyond story. It is even beyond words, outside language. That is its point, or at least its strongest claim: that it cannot be described. But since when did "the indescribable" ever stop a writer?

The most convincing and enduring testaments of mystical union in the Christian tradition turn for method, it seems instinctively and against the let-me-be-lost-in-You-oh-Lord claims of the writer, to the ways and means of autobiography. Perhaps it must be so: on this subject, personal experience alone is authority and intimate testimony the only thing that counts as expertise. No detached investigator can assess and no objective journalist can accurately "report" on transcendence. We're stuck with the claim of a first person account.

In fact, autobiography, a form that in our day bristles with sharply secular and psychological concerns, traces its literary taproot to Augustine's attempt, begun in 397, to struggle the angel of mystical union unto the mat of the page in his *Confessions*. Nor is Augustine alone. The history of Western autobiography is punctuated by such religious accounts, as if the very insubstantiality of spiritual life were, paradoxically, the real subject of any examined life, the engine powering every personal story.

After Augustine, there is the "great" Teresa of Avila's *Autobiography*, another classic of Western autobiographical literature. In modern times the slim The Story of a Soul by Thérèse of Lisieux—"The Little Flower," as she is known to distinguish her more childlike spirituality from that of the mature Teresa— remains a perennial best-seller. The personal accounts of such unsettling twentieth century mystics as Simone Weil and Edith Stein also retain a hold over the imaginations of readers, religious or not. Describing the indescribable by using their own lives as their only evidence, these spiritual writers cannot stray far from personal testimony. Augustine, Teresa and Thérèse, Edith Stein, Simone Weil—all mystics, all memoirists.

The Interior Castle is in effect an anti-memoir. It is Teresa's second try (over a decade after her 1565 Autobiography) at describing the galvanizing, subliminally erotic communion with the divine that is her radical spiritual legacy within Christianity. But unlike the Autobiography, this later book is not a personal story. Teresa even employs patently transparent locutions like "I know a person who . . ." to put a scrim between herself and her testimony.

Both the Autobiography and The Interior Castle were undertaken at the request, really the command, of her religious directors. They were probably partly written as prudent defenses against the ever-vigilant Inquisition. Mystical prayer may not strike the secular modern as a particularly dangerous political enterprise— compared, say, to a direct critique of the ruling structures of the prevailing powers of church or state.

Yet as orthodoxies of all kinds at all times understand very well, it is precisely the interior experience of personal coherence—felt as integrity—that makes individuals virtually impossible to control en masse. Nor is this religious unruliness a lost figment of history. Think only of China's response to the Falun Gong movement: Can a lot of people, many of them elderly, doing breathing exercises in public while waving their arms above their heads really pose a threat to the governing orthodoxy, well-armed and in charge of the power structures though it is? Well, yes.

Teresa, like all mystics, attests not only to the wonder of God's love but to the divinity residing within each individual. This is a volatile assertion, and in a paradox often missed in our secular world (at least until 9/11), interior prayer and mystical experience can be serious political threats. Christianity, though ironically enough a religion based precisely on this notion of God-made-Man, has been particularly nervous about promoting the interior experience of religious union. The Church's motto has long seemed to be: do not try this at home alone. For if interior prayer is based on a loose federation of seekers and "spiritual directors" or "guides," then what happens to Christendom with its structures and hierarchies?

Teresa's *Castle* is a handbook on mysticism, written for her sisters, but really useful to any serious lay practitioner, a sort of proto–self-help book for contemplatives, in the spirit of the anonymous English medieval tract *The Cloud of Unknowing*. But of course Teresa is not an anonymous author and all her fluttering of fans before her own face—"a certain person I know," "one woman who"—cannot keep her ardent personality off the page, no matter that she has attempted to efface herself as she attempts to present, instead of another autobiography, a practical guide for other aspiring contemplatives.

Mystical experience may not lend itself to narrative, but it is more than half in love with poetry. Teresa's text positively dances with metaphor—her primary figure of speech of course is her vision of the "interior castle," the image upon which the whole book and its contemplative model is based. In Spanish known as "The Mansions," these seven locations are stages in the inward progress of the contemplative to ultimate union. This is the unreal estate of the spirit.

It is interesting to note that in a tradition as skyward and vertical—and hierarchical—as Teresa's Catholicism, her natural figure for this progress of transcendence is not upward but inward, penetrating even, to the inmost regions of the "palace where the king lives." The soul is "a paradise where the Lord says he finds his delight." And the body—always a vexing limitation to the mystic—is but "the outer walls of the castle." Self-knowledge is "a room," and the aspirant is instructed always to "visualize your soul as vast, spacious, and plentiful. This amplitude is impossible to exaggerate."

In her ceaseless image-making Teresa bears a certain kinship with Rumi, the glorious Sufi poet. Both of them delight in invoking lovemaking as the metaphor that best captures the sensation of spiritual ecstasy. "Imagine a palmetto fruit," she says. "Layer upon layer must be peeled away to reach the tasty part in the middle. So it is with the interior castle. Many rooms surround the central chamber."

In the Seventh and final Dwelling Places, the ultimate arrival of spiritual intimacy between God and self, Teresa turns, as if inevitably, to the metaphor of marriage. And she does not mean a modest domestic arrangement, but the passionate merging of love, the union of beloveds.

In an age—our own—when the treasures of Catholic spirituality often seem to be eclipsed in the popular mind by the brittle restrictions and prohibitions of the institutional Church (no gays, no women priests) and the shameful subterfuges of the sex abuse scandal, it is indeed like entering a "vast, spacious, and plentiful" chamber to read Teresa's evergreen masterpiece of the searching heart.

Here body and soul find perfect register with their God in the metaphor of the spousal embrace within the inmost chamber of the crystal palace. Here, Teresa assures us, past all the struggles, all the serpents and "beasts" that beset the long courtship, we arrive at "a secret place where His Majesty has taken the soul and unveiled himself to her."

—PATRICIA HAMPL

INTRODUCTION

I first studied Teresa of Avila's *Interior Castle* twenty or so years ago, after many years of efforts to understand, live, and communicate what the spiritual life portrayed in the Bible was meant to be. I had found many helpful companions on the Way, spread across time and space and denominational distinctions. But this book and this author immediately announced themselves as a unique presence of God in my life. *The Interior Castle* provided instruction on how to have a living relationship with God that I had found nowhere else. I think it very likely that you will experience the same refreshing shock as I did when you read this book.

The first thing that Teresa helped me with was appreciation of the dignity and value—indeed, the vast reality—of the human soul. Emphasis upon the wickedness and neediness of the human being tends to submerge our awareness of our greatness and our worth to God. This emphasis in turn inclines us toward thinking of ourselves as *nothing*—to mistake our lostness and vileness for nothingness, a mere vacuum, rather than seeing it as the desolation of a *splendid ruin*.

Teresa urges us to start on the path to transformation by "considering our soul to be like a castle made entirely out of a diamond or of very clear crystal, in which there are many rooms." We are meant to occupy every room or "dwelling place" with God, and thereby to become the radiant beings which he intends. Teresa makes clear what lies half-concealed upon the pages of the Bible and in the lives of the "great ones" for Christ—that we are unceasing spiritual beings, with an eternal destiny in God's great universe. We may be far from God's will, but we must know "that it is possible in this exile for so great a God to commune with such foul-smelling worms; and, on seeing this, come to love a goodness so perfect and a mercy so immeasurable."

The "rooms" in the interior castle are ways of living in relation to the God who made us and seeks us. Teresa's superiors had ordered her to write on prayer. And so she does, but prayer understood precisely as a way of living, not as an occasional exercise. This book, and others, such as *The Way of the Pilgrim*, helped me to understand what it is to live a life of prayer. I learned what it means to live in communication with God—not just in speaking but in listening and acting. Most of what I know about the phenomenology of God's communication, I learned from studying and putting into practice what Teresa says in Chapter Three of the Sixth Dwelling Places. It is still, I think, the best treatment ever written of what it is like for God to *speak* to his children.

Another thing I came to see more clearly was why things develop as they do in the spiritual lives of professing Christians. There is still today not much good information on this. But if you look at ordinary "church life" with the First through Fourth Dwelling Places in hand, you will be able to understand a huge amount of what is really going on, and of what to expect, for good and for ill. You will be able to give good counsel and direction to yourself and others as you go through the process of life together. Teresa is an absolute master of the spiritual life and possesses an amazing depth and richness of spiritual theology. Yet there is no stuffiness or mere "head knowledge" in her at all. She has remarkable freedom to be experimental, and to say "now I can't really explain this to you," but to go ahead and say astonishingly illuminating things anyway. You can put what she says to the test.

Behind all of this instruction is the suggestion (which was very important for my particular background) that there is a reliable order and sequence to growth in the spiritual life. This is built into her model of the "castle" of the soul. "Now," she in effect says, "this is the layout, this is what is to be gone through, here is where you start, here are some things to do, and here is what you may expect to happen and what it means." And she conveys all this wisdom with an appealing, humble tone.

Finally, the Fifth through Seventh Dwelling Places proved to be, for me, the finest treatments of union with Christ and with God that I have found in spiritual literature. There are other helpful readings on this connection, such as James Stewart's *A Man in Christ*, but for the phenomenology, the descriptive analysis of what this union is really like, nothing has ever surpassed Teresa's *Castle*. Union with Christ—in regeneration, justification, sanctification, and glorification—is of all themes the one in most need of recovery today. And Teresa's entire treatment of redemption in the spiritual life with Christ is unsurpassed and unlikely to be surpassed in the future.

One of the unfortunate things that has happened to the latter stages of *The Interior Castle*, and even to the book as a whole, is that people have tried to read it as if it were an "interfaith," not a distinctively Christian, portrayal of "mystic union." To do this is to miss its substance and deprive it of its context. Of course anyone is free to take what they can from it, but to dismiss its particularity will leave little to genuinely assist the reader to walk with God.

A suggestion about how to read this book. It is not easy reading and must be approached as if you were mining for treasure—which you are. First, read it nonstop—just push ahead—to get a view of the whole. Mark themes and divisions clearly as you go, and at the end sketch out the outline. This is crucial for under-standing Teresa's project as a teacher. Then go back and read slowly from beginning to end. This time, mark striking passages for fur-ther study. Then meditatively dwell on those passages, not necessar-ily from beginning to end, but in the order your heart and mind call you to. Call upon "His Majesty" to assist you as he assisted Teresa. And the "diamond castle" of your own soul will increas-ingly glow with the divine presence.

—DALLAS WILLARD

PROLOGUE

Teresa of Jesus, a nun of Our Lady of Mount Carmel, wrote this treatise for her sisters and daughters, the Discalced Carmelite nuns.

Not many things that I have been ordered to do under obedience have been as difficult for me as is this present task of writing about prayer. First, it doesn't seem that the Lord is giving me either the spirit or the desire to undertake the work. Second, I have been experiencing now for three months such great noise and weakness in my head that I've found it a hardship even to write concerning necessary business matters. But, knowing that the strength given by obedience usually lessens the difficulty of things that seem impossible, I resolved to carry out the task very willingly, even though my human nature seems greatly distressed. For the Lord hasn't given me so much virtue that my nature in the midst of its struggle with continual sickness and duties of so many kinds doesn't feel strong aversion toward such a task. May he, in whose mercy I trust and who has helped me in other, more difficult things so as to favor me, do this work for me.

Indeed, I don't think I have much more to say than what I've said in other things they have ordered me to write; rather, I fear that the things I write about will be nearly all alike. I'm, literally, just like the parrots that are taught to speak; they know no more than what they hear or are shown, and they often repeat it. If the Lord wants me to say something new, His Majesty will provide. Or he will be pleased to make me remember what I have said at other times, for I would be happy even with this. My memory is so poor that I would be glad if I could repeat, in case they've been lost, some of the things that I was told were well said. If the Lord doesn't make me remember, I will gain just by tiring myself and getting a worse headache for the sake of obedience—even though no benefit will be drawn from what I say.

And so I'm beginning to comply today, the feast of the most Blessed Trinity, in the year 1577, in this Carmelite monastery of St. Joseph in Toledo, where I am at present. In all that I say I submit to the opinion of the ones who ordered me to write, for they are persons of great learning. If I should say something that isn't in conformity with what the holy Roman Catholic Church holds, it will be through ignorance and not through malice. This can be held as certain, and also that through the goodness of God I always am, and will be, and have been subject to her. May he be always blessed and glorified, amen.

The one who ordered me to write told me that the nuns in these monasteries of Our Lady of Mount Carmel need someone to answer their questions about prayer and that he thought they would better understand the language used between women, and that because of the love they bore me, they would pay more attention to what I would tell them. I thus understood that it was important for me to manage to say something. So I shall be speaking to them while I write; it's nonsense to think that what I say could matter to other persons. Our Lord will be granting me favor enough if some of these nuns benefit by praising him a little more. His Majesty well knows that I don't aim for anything else. And it should be very clear that if I manage to say something well, the sisters will understand that this does not come from me, since there would be no foundation for it unless the Lord gave it to me; otherwise they would have as little intelligence as I ability for such things.

THE FIRST
DWELLING PLACES

Chapter 1

Discusses the beauty and dignity of our souls.
Draws a comparison in order to explain, and speaks
of the benefit that comes from understanding this truth
and knowing about the favors we receive
from God and how the door to this castle is
prayer.

Today while beseeching our Lord to speak for me because I wasn't able to think of anything to say nor did I know how to begin to carry out this obedience, there came to my mind what I shall now speak about, that which will provide us with a basis to begin with. It is that we consider our soul to be like a castle made entirely out of a diamond or of very clear crystal, in which there are many rooms, just as in heaven there are many dwelling places [John 14:2]. For in reflecting upon it carefully, sisters, we realize that the soul of the just person is nothing else but a paradise where the Lord says he finds his delight. So then, what do you think that abode will be like where a King so powerful, so wise, so pure, so full of all good things takes his delight? [Prov. 8:31]. I don't find anything comparable to the magnificent beauty of a soul and its marvelous capacity. Indeed, our intellects, however keen, can hardly comprehend it, just as they cannot comprehend God; but he himself says that he created us in his own image and likeness [Gen. 1:26–27].

Well, if this is true, as it is, there is no reason to tire ourselves in trying to comprehend the beauty of this castle. Since this castle is a creature and the difference, therefore, between it and God is the same as that between the Creator and his creature, His Majesty in saying that the soul is made in his own image makes it almost impossible for us to understand the sublime dignity and beauty of the soul.

It is a shame and unfortunate that through our own fault we don't understand ourselves or know who we are. Wouldn't it show great ignorance, my daughters, if someone, when asked who he was, didn't know, and didn't know his father or mother or from what country he came? Well, now, if this would be so extremely stupid, we are incomparably more so when we do not strive to know who we are, but limit ourselves to considering only roughly these bodies. Because we have heard and because faith tells us so, we know we have souls. But we seldom consider the precious things that can be found in this soul, or who dwells within it, or its high value. Consequently, little effort is made to preserve its beauty. All our attention is taken up with the plainness of the diamond's setting or the outer wall of the castle, that is, with these bodies of ours.

Well, let us consider that this castle has, as I said, many dwelling places: some up above, others down below, others to the sides; and in the center and middle is the main dwelling place where the very secret exchanges between God and the soul take place.

It's necessary that you keep this comparison in mind. Perhaps God will be pleased to let me use it to explain something to you about the favors he is happy to grant souls and the differences between these favors. I shall explain them according to what I have understood as possible. For it is impossible that anyone understand them all, since there are many; how much more so for someone as wretched as I. It will be a great consolation when the Lord grants them to you if you know that they are possible; and for anyone to whom he doesn't, it will be a great consolation to praise his wonderful goodness. Just as it doesn't do us any harm to reflect on the things there are in heaven and what the blessed enjoy—but, rather, we rejoice and strive to attain what they enjoy—it doesn't do us any harm to see that it is possible in this exile for so great a God to commune with such foul-smelling worms; and, on seeing this, come to love a goodness so perfect and a mercy so immeasurable. I hold as certain that anyone who might be harmed by knowing that God can grant this favor in this exile would be very much lacking in humility and love of neighbor. Otherwise, how could we fail to be happy that God grants these favors to our brother? His doing so is no impediment toward his granting them to us, and His Majesty can reveal his grandeurs to whomever he wants. Sometimes he does so merely to show forth his glory, as he said of the blind man whose sight he restored when his apostles asked him if the blindness resulted from the man's sins or those of his parents [John 9:2–3]. Hence, he doesn't grant them because the sanctity of the recipients is greater than that of those who don't receive them, but so that his glory may be known, as we see in St. Paul and the Magdalene, and that we might praise him for his work in creatures.

One could say that these favors seem to be impossible and that it is good not to scandalize the weak. Less is lost when the weak do not believe in them than when the favors fail to benefit those to whom God grants them; and these latter will be delighted and awakened through these favors to a greater love of him who grants so many gifts and whose power and majesty are so great. Moreover, I know I am speaking to those for whom this danger does not exist, for they know and believe that God grants even greater signs of his love. I know that whoever does not believe in these favors will have no experience of them, for God doesn't like us to put a limit on his works. And so, sisters, those of you whom the Lord doesn't lead by this path should never doubt his generosity.

Well, getting back to our beautiful and delightful castle, we must see how we can enter it. It seems I'm saying something foolish. For if this castle is the soul, clearly one doesn't have to enter it since it is within oneself. How foolish it would seem were we to tell someone to enter a room he is already in. But you must understand that there is a great difference in the ways one may be inside the castle. For there are many souls who are in the outer courtyard—which is where the guards stay—and don't care at all about entering the castle, nor do they know what lies within that most precious place, nor who is within, nor even how many rooms it has. You have already heard in some books on prayer that the soul is advised to enter within itself; well, that's the very thing I'm advising.

Not long ago a very learned man told me that souls who do not practice prayer are like people with paralyzed or crippled bodies;

even though they have hands and feet, they cannot give orders to these hands and feet. Thus there are souls so ill and so accustomed to being involved in external matters that there is no remedy, nor does it seem they can enter within themselves. They are now so used to dealing always with the insects and vermin that are in the wall surrounding the castle that they have become almost like them. And though they have so rich a nature and the power to converse with none other than God, there is no remedy. If these souls do not strive to understand and cure their great misery, they will be changed into statues of salt, unable to turn their heads to look at themselves, just as Lot's wife was changed for having turned her head [Gen. 19:26].

Insofar as I can understand, the gate of entry to this castle is prayer and reflection. I don't mean to refer to mental more than vocal prayer, for since vocal prayer is prayer it must be accompanied by reflection. A prayer in which a person is not aware of whom he is speaking to, what he is asking, or who it is who is asking and of whom I do not call prayer, however much the lips may move. Sometimes it will be so without this reflection, provided that the soul has these reflections at other times. Nonetheless, anyone who has the habit of speaking before God's majesty as though he were speaking to a slave, without being careful to see how he is speaking, but saying whatever comes to his head and whatever he has learned from saying at other times, in my opinion is not praying. Please God, may no Christian pray in this way. Among yourselves, sisters, I hope in His Majesty that you will not do so, for the custom you have of being occupied with interior things is quite a good safeguard against falling and carrying on in this way like brute beasts.

Well, now, we are not speaking to these crippled souls, for if the Lord himself doesn't come to order them to get up—as he did the man who waited at the side of the pool for thirty years [John 5:5]—they are quite unfortunate and in serious danger. But we are speaking to other souls that, in the end, enter the castle. For even though they are very involved in the world, they have good desires and sometimes, though only once in a while, they entrust themselves to our Lord and reflect on who they are, although in a rather hurried fashion. During the period of a month they will sometimes pray, but their minds are then filled with business matters that ordinarily occupy them. They are so attached to these things that, where their treasure lies, their heart goes also [Matt. 6:21]. Sometimes they do put all these things aside, and the self-knowledge and awareness that they are not proceeding correctly in order to get to the door is important. Finally, they enter the first, lower rooms. But so many reptiles get in with them that they are prevented from seeing the beauty of the castle and from calming down; they have done quite a bit just by having entered.

You may have been thinking, daughters, that this is irrelevant to you since by the Lord's goodness you are not among these people. You'll have to have patience, for I wouldn't know how to explain my understanding of some interior things about prayer if not in this way. And may it even please the Lord that I succeed in saying something, for what I want to explain to you is very difficult to understand without experience. If you have experience you will see that one cannot avoid touching upon things that—please God, through his mercy—do not pertain to us.

THE SECOND
DWELLING PLACES

Chapter 1

Discusses the importance of perseverance
if one is to reach the final dwelling places; the
great war the devil wages; and the importance
of taking the right road from the beginning.
Offers a remedy that has proved very
efficacious.

Now let us speak about the type of soul that enters the second dwelling places and what such a soul does in them. I'd like to say only a little, for I have spoken at length on this subject elsewhere. And it would be impossible to avoid repeating much of it, for I don't remember a thing of what I said. If I could present the matter for you in a variety of ways, I know well that you wouldn't be annoyed, since we never tire of books—as many as there are—that deal with it.

This stage pertains to those who have already begun to practice prayer and have understood how important it is not to stay in the first dwelling places. But they still don't have the determination to remain in this second stage without turning back, for they don't avoid the occasions of sin. This failure to avoid these occasions is quite dangerous. But these persons have received a good deal of mercy in that they sometimes do strive to escape from snakes and poisonous creatures, and they understand that it is good to avoid them.

These rooms, in part, involve much more effort than do the first, even though there is not as much danger, for it now seems that souls in them recognize the dangers, and there is great hope they will enter farther into the castle. I say that these rooms involve more effort because those who are in the first dwelling places are like deaf-mutes, and thus the difficulty of not speaking is more easily endured by them than it is by those who hear but cannot speak. Yet not for this reason does one have greater desire to be deaf, for after all it is a wonderful thing to hear what is being said to us. So these persons are able to hear the Lord's callings. Since they are getting closer to where His Majesty dwells, he is a very good neighbor. His mercy and goodness are so bountiful, whereas we are occupied in our pastimes, business affairs, pleasures, and worldly buying and selling, and still falling into sin and rising again. These beasts are so poisonous and their presence so dangerous and noisy that it would be a wonder if we kept from stumbling and falling over them. Yet this Lord desires intensely that we love him and seek his company, so much so that from time to time he calls us to draw near him. And his voice is so sweet the poor soul dissolves at not doing immediately what he commands. Thus, as I say, hearing his voice is a greater trial than not hearing it.

I don't mean that these appeals and calls are like the ones I shall speak of later on. But they come through words spoken by other good people, or through sermons, or through what is read in good books, or through the many things that are heard and by which God calls, or through illnesses and trials, or also through a truth that he teaches during the brief moments we spend in prayer; however lukewarm these moments may be, God esteems them highly. And you, sisters, don't underestimate this first favor, nor should you become disconsolate if you don't respond at once to the Lord. His Majesty knows well how to wait many days and years, especially when he sees perseverance and good desires. This perseverance is most necessary here. One always gains much through perseverance. But the attacks made by devils in a thousand ways afflict the soul more in these rooms than in the previous ones. In the previous ones the soul was deaf and dumb—at least it heard very little and resisted less, as one who has partly lost hope of conquering. Here the intellect is more alive and the faculties more skilled. The blows from the artillery strike in such a way that the soul cannot fail to hear. It is in this stage that the devils represent these snakes (worldly things) and the temporal pleasures of the present as though almost eternal. They bring to mind the esteem one has in the world, one's friends and relatives, one's health (when there's thought of penitential practices, for the soul that enters this dwelling place always begins wanting to practice some penance), and a thousand other obstacles.

O Jesus, what an uproar the devils instigate here! And the afflictions of the poor soul: it doesn't know whether to continue or to return to the first room. Reason, for its part, shows the soul that it is mistaken in thinking that these things of the world are not worth anything when compared to what it is aiming after. Faith, however, teaches it about where it will find fulfillment. The memory shows it where all these things end, holding before it the death of those who found great joy in them. Through the memory it sees how some have suffered sudden death, how quickly they are forgotten by all. Some whom it had known in great prosperity are under the ground, and their graves are walked on. This soul itself has often passed by these graves. It reflects that many worms are swarming over the corpses and thinks about numerous other things. The will is inclined to love after seeing such countless signs of love; it would want to repay something; it especially keeps in mind how this true Lover never leaves it, accompanying it and giving it life and being. Then the intellect helps it realize that it couldn't find a better friend, even were it to live for many years; that the whole world is filled with falsehood; and that so too these joys the devil gives it are filled with trials, cares, and contradictions. The intellect tells the soul of its certainty that outside this castle neither security nor peace will be found, that it should avoid going about to strange houses, since its own is so filled with blessings to be enjoyed if it wants. The intellect will ask who it is that finds everything he needs in his own house and, especially, has a guest who will make him lord over all goods, provided that he wills to avoid going astray like the prodigal son and eating the husks of swine [Luke 15:16].

These are reasons for conquering the devils. But, O my Lord and my God, how the whole world's habit of getting involved in vanities vitiates everything! Our faith is so dead that we desire what we see more than what faith tells us. And, indeed, we see only a lot of misfortune in those who go after these visible vanities. But these poisonous things we are dealing with are the cause of this misfortune, for just as all is poisoned if a viper bites someone and the wound swells, so we will be poisoned if we do not watch ourselves. Clearly many remedies are necessary to cure us, and God is favoring us a good deal if we do not die from the wound. Certainly the soul undergoes great trials here; and especially if the devil realizes that it has all it needs in its temperament and habits to advance far, he will gather all hell together to make the soul go back outside.

O my Lord! Your help is necessary here; without it one can do nothing [John 15:5]. In your mercy do not consent to allow this soul to suffer deception and give up what was begun. Enlighten it that it may see how all its good is within this castle and that it may turn away from bad companions. It's a wonderful thing for a person to talk to those who speak about this interior castle, to draw near not only to those seen to be in these rooms where he is, but to those known to have entered the ones closer to the center. Conversation with these latter will be a great help to him, and he can converse so much with them that they will bring him to where they are. Let the soul always heed the warning not to be conquered. If the devil sees that it has the strong determination to lose its life and repose and all that he offers it rather than return to the first room, he will abandon it much more quickly. Let the soul be manly and not like those soldiers who knelt down to drink before going into battle (I don't remember with whom) [Judg. 7:5], but be determined to fight with all the devils and realize that there are no better weapons than those of the cross.

Even though I've said this at other times, it's so important that I repeat it here: it is that souls shouldn't be thinking about consolations at this beginning stage. It would be a very poor way to start building so precious and great an edifice. If the foundation is on sand, the whole building will fall to the ground. They'll never finish being dissatisfied and tempted. These are not the dwelling places where it rains manna; those lie farther ahead, where a soul finds in the manna every taste it desires [Wis. 16:20]; for it wants only what God wants. It's an amusing thing that even though we still have a thousand impediments and imperfections and our virtues have hardly begun to grow—and please God they may have begun—we are yet not ashamed to seek spiritual delights in prayer or to complain about dryness. May this never happen to you, sisters. Embrace the cross your Spouse has carried and understand that this must be your task. Let the one who can do so suffer more for him, and she will be rewarded that much more. As for other favors, if the Lord should grant you one, thank him for it as you would for something freely added on.

It will seem to you that you are truly determined to undergo exterior trials, provided that God favors you interiorly. His Majesty knows best what is suitable for us. There's no need for us to be advising him about what he should give us, for he can rightly tell us that we don't know what we're asking for [Matt. 20:22]. The whole aim of any person who is beginning prayer— and don't forget this, because it's very important—should be that he work and prepare himself with determination and every possible effort to bring his will into conformity with God's will. Be certain that, as I shall say later, the greatest perfection attainable along the spiritual path lies in this conformity. It is the person who lives in more perfect conformity who will receive more from the Lord and be more advanced on this road. Don't think that, in what concerns perfection, there is some mystery or things unknown or still to be understood, for in perfect conformity to God's will lies all our good. Now then, if we err in the beginning, desiring that the Lord do our will at once and lead us according to what we imagine, what kind of stability will this edifice have? Let us strive to do what lies in our power and guard ourselves against these poisonous little reptiles, for the Lord often desires that dryness and bad thoughts afflict and pursue us without our being able to get rid of them. Sometimes he even permits these reptiles to bite us, so that afterward we may know how to guard ourselves better and that he may prove whether we are greatly grieved by having offended him.

Thus, if you should at times fall, don't become discouraged and stop striving to advance. For even from this fall God will draw out good, as does the seller of an antidote who drinks some poison in order to test whether his antidote is effective. Even if we didn't see our misery—or the great harm that a dissipated life does to us— through any other means than through this assault that we endure for the sake of being brought back to recollection, that would be enough. Can there be an evil greater than that of being ill at ease in our own house? What hope can we have of finding rest outside of ourselves if we cannot be at rest within? We have so many great and true friends and relatives (which are our faculties) with whom we must always live, even though we may not want to. But from what we feel, these seem to be warring against us because of what our vices have done to them. "Peace, peace," the Lord said, my sisters; and he urged his apostle so many times [John 20:19–21]. Well, believe me, if we don't obtain and have peace in our own house, we'll not find it outside. Let this war be ended. Through the blood he shed for us I ask those who have not begun to enter within themselves to do so; and those who have begun not to let the war make them turn back. Let these latter reflect that a relapse is worse than a fall; they already see their loss. Let them trust in the mercy of God and not at all in themselves, and they will see how His Majesty brings them from the dwelling places of one stage to those of another and settles them in a land where these wild animals cannot touch or tire them, but where they themselves will bring all these animals into subjection and scoff at them. And they shall enjoy many more blessings than one can desire—blessings even in this life, I mean.

Since, as I've said in the beginning, I've written to you about how you should conduct yourselves in these disturbances set up here by the devil and how you cannot begin to recollect yourselves by force, but only by gentleness, if your recollection is going to be more continual, I will not say anything else here other than that, in my opinion, it is very important to consult persons with experience; for you will be thinking that you are seriously failing to do some necessary thing. Provided that we don't give up, the Lord will guide everything for our benefit, even though we may not find someone to teach us. There is no other remedy for this evil of giving up prayer than to begin again; otherwise the soul will gradually lose more each day—and please God that it will understand this fact.

Someone could think that, if turning back is so bad, it would be better never to begin, but to remain outside the castle. I have already told you at the beginning—and the Lord himself tells you—that anyone who walks in danger perishes in it [Sir. 3:26], and that the door of entry to this castle is prayer. Well, now, it is foolish to think that we will enter heaven without entering into ourselves, coming to know ourselves, reflecting on our misery and what we owe God, and begging him often for mercy. The Lord himself says: "No one will ascend to my Father but through me" [John 14:6] (I don't know if he says it this way—I think he does) and "Whoever sees me sees my Father" [John 14:9]. Well, if we never look at him or reflect on what we owe him and the death he suffered for us, I don't know how we'll be able to know him or do works in his service. And what value can faith have without works and without joining them to the merits of Jesus Christ, our Good? Or who will awaken us to love this Lord?

May it please His Majesty to give us understanding of how much we cost him, of how the servant is no greater than his master [Matt. 10:24], and that we must work in order to enjoy his glory. And we need to pray for this understanding, so that we aren't always entering into temptation [Matt. 26:41].

THE THIRD
DWELLING PLACES

Chapter 1

*Treats what little security we can have
while living in this exile, even though we may
have reached a high state, and how we should
walk with fear. This chapter has some good
points.*

What shall we say to those who through perseverance and the mercy of God have won these battles and have entered the rooms of the third stage, if not: "Blessed is the man who fears the Lord" [Ps. 112:1]? His Majesty has done no small thing in giving me understanding right now of what this verse means in the vernacular, for I am ignorant in matters like this. Certainly we are right in calling such a man blessed, since if he doesn't turn back he is, from what we can understand, on the secure path to his salvation. Here you will see, sisters, how important it was to win the previous battles. I am certain the Lord never fails to give a person like this security of conscience, which is no small blessing. I said "security" and I was wrong, for there is no security in this life; so always understand that I mean "if he doesn't abandon the path he began on."

It is a great misery to have to live a life in which we must always walk like those whose enemies are at their doorstep; they can neither sleep nor eat without weapons and without being always frightened lest somewhere these enemies might be able to break through this fortress. O my Lord and my Good, how is it that you want us to desire so miserable a life, for it isn't possible to stop wanting and asking you to take us out of it unless there is hope of losing it for you or of spending it very earnestly in your service or, above all, of understanding what your will is? If it is your will, my God, may we die with you, as St. Thomas said [John 11:16]; for living without you and with these fears of the possibility of losing you forever is nothing else than dying often. That's why, daughters, I say that the blessedness we must ask for is that of being already secure with the blessed. For with these fears, what happiness can anyone have whose whole happiness is to please God? Consider that this happiness was had—and in much greater degree—by some saints who fell into serious sins and that we are not sure that God will help us to get free from these sins and to do penance for them.

Certainly, my daughters, I am so fearful as I write this that I don't know how I'm writing it or how I live when I think about it, which is very often. Pray, my daughters, that His Majesty may live in me always. If he doesn't, what security can a life as badly spent as mine have? And do not become sad in knowing that this life has been badly spent, as I have sometimes observed you become when I tell this to you; you continue to desire that I might have lived a very holy life—and you are right. I too would want to have so lived, but what can I do if I have lost holiness through my own fault! I will not complain about God, who gave me enough help to carry out your desires. I cannot say this without tears and without being very ashamed that I am writing something for those who can teach me. Doing so has been a hard command to obey! May it please the Lord that, since it is being done for him, it may be of some benefit to you, so that you may ask him to pardon this miserable and bold creature. But His Majesty well knows that I can boast only of his mercy, and since I cannot cease being what I have been, I have no other remedy than to approach his mercy and to trust in the merits of his Son and of the Virgin, his mother, whose habit I wear so unworthily, and you wear. Praise him, my daughters, for you truly belong to Our Lady. Thus you have no reason to be ashamed of my misery, since you have such a good Mother. Imitate her and reflect that the grandeur of Our Lady and the good of having her for your patroness must be indeed great, since my sins and my being what I am have not been enough to tarnish in any way this sacred order.

But one thing I advise you: not because you have such a Mother or patroness should you feel secure, for David was very holy, and you already know who Solomon was. Don't pay any attention to the enclosure and the penance in which you live, or feel safe in the fact that you are always conversing with God and practicing such continual prayer and being so withdrawn from the world of things and, in your opinion, holding them in abhorrence. These practices are all good, but not a sufficient reason, as I have said, for us to stop fearing. So continue to say this verse and often bear it in mind: *Beatus vir qui timet Dominum* ("Blessed is the man who fears the Lord").

I don't remember what I was speaking about, for I have digressed a great deal and in thinking of myself I feel helpless, as a bird with broken wings, when it comes to saying anything good.

So I want to leave this matter aside for now. Let me get back to what I began telling you concerning souls that have entered the third dwelling places, for the Lord has done them no small favor, but a very great one, in letting them get through the first difficulties. I believe that through the goodness of God there are many of these souls in the world. They long not to offend His Majesty, even guarding themselves against venial sins; they are fond of doing penance and setting aside periods for recollection; they spend their time well, practicing works of charity toward their neighbors, and are very balanced in their use of speech and dress and in the governing of their households—those who have them. Certainly, this is a state to be desired. And, in my opinion, there is no reason why entrance even into the final dwelling place should be denied these souls, nor will the Lord deny them this entrance if they desire it; for such a desire is an excellent way to prepare oneself so that every favor may be granted.

O Jesus, and who will say that he doesn't want a good so wonderful, especially after having passed through the most difficult trial? No, nobody will. We all say that we want this good. But since there is need of still more in order that the soul possess the Lord completely, it is not enough to say we want it, just as this was not enough for the young man whom the Lord told what one must do in order to be perfect [Matt. 19:16–22]. From the time I began to speak of these dwelling places, I have had this young man in mind. For we are literally like him, and ordinarily the great dryness in prayer comes from this, although it also has

other causes. And I'm leaving aside mention of some interior trials that many good souls undergo (unbearable trials and not at all
due to their own fault), from which the Lord always frees them
to their own great benefit, and mention of those who suffer from
melancholy and other illnesses. Briefly, in all things we have to let
God be the judge. What I've said, I believe, is what usually happens; for since these souls realize that they wouldn't commit a
sin for anything—many wouldn't even advertently commit a
venial sin—and that they conduct their lives and households
well, they cannot accept patiently that the door of entry to the
place where our King dwells be closed to them who consider
themselves his vassals. But even though a king here on earth has
many vassals, not all enter his chamber. Enter, enter, my daughters, into the interior rooms; pass on from your little works. By
the mere fact that you are Christians you must do all these things
and much more. It is enough for you to be God's vassals; don't
let your desire be for so much that, as a result, you will be left
with nothing. Behold the saints who entered this King's chamber,
and you will see the difference between them and us. Don't ask
for what you have not deserved, nor should it enter our minds
that we have merited this favor however much we may have
served—we who have offended God.

   O humility, humility! I don't know what kind of temptation
I'm undergoing in this matter that I cannot help but think that
anyone who makes such an issue of this dryness is a little lacking
in humility. I said that I've omitted mention of those great interior trials I've referred to, for those involve much more than just a

lack of devotion. Let us prove ourselves, my sisters, or let the Lord prove us, for he knows well how to do this, even though we often don't want to understand it. Let us speak now of those souls whose lives are so well ordered; let us recognize what they do for God, and we shall at once see how we have no reason for complaining of His Majesty. If, like the young man in the gospel, we turn our backs and go away sad when the Lord tells us what we must do to be perfect, what do you want His Majesty to do? For he must give the reward in conformity with the love we have for him. And this love, daughters, must not be fabricated in our imaginations, but proved by deeds. And don't think he needs our works; he needs the determination of our wills.

We seem to think that everything is done when we willingly take and wear the religious habit and abandon all worldly things and possessions for him—even though these possessions may amount to no more than the nets St. Peter possessed [Matt. 19:27]—for he who gives what he has thinks he gives enough. This renunciation is a good enough preparation, if one perseveres in it and doesn't turn back and become involved with the vermin in the first rooms, even if it be only in desire. There is no doubt that, if a person perseveres in this nakedness and detachment from all worldly things, he will reach his goal. But this perseverance includes the condition—and behold that I am advising you of this—that you consider yourselves useless servants, as St. Paul or Christ says [Luke 17:10], and believe that you have not put our Lord under any obligation to grant you these kinds of favors. Rather, as one who has received more, you are more indebted

[Luke 12:48]. What can we do for a God so generous that he died for us, created us, and gives us being? Shouldn't we consider ourselves lucky to be able to repay something of what we owe him for his service toward us? I say these words "his service toward us" unwillingly; but the fact is that he did nothing else but serve us all the time he lived in this world. And yet we ask him again for favors and gifts.

Reflect a great deal, daughters, on some of the things that are here pointed out, even though in a jumbled way, for I don't know how to explain them further. The Lord will give you understanding of them, so that out of dryness you may draw humility—and not disquiet, which is what the devil aims for. Be convinced that where humility is truly present God will give a peace and conformity—even though he may never give consolations—by which one will walk with greater contentment than will others with their consolations. For often, as you have read, the divine Majesty gives these consolations to the weaker souls, although I think we would not exchange these consolations for the fortitude of those who walk in dryness. We are fonder of consolations than we are of the cross. Test us, Lord—for you know the truth—so that we may know ourselves.

THE FOURTH
DWELLING PLACES

Chapter 2

Continues on the same subject and explains
through a comparison the nature of spiritual
delight and how this is attained by not
seeking it.

God help me with what I have undertaken! I've already forgotten what I was dealing with, for business matters and poor health have forced me to set this work aside just when I was at my best; and since I have a poor memory, everything will come out confused, because I can't go back to read it over. And perhaps even everything else I say is confused; at least that's what I feel it is.

It seems to me I have explained the nature of consolations in the spiritual life. Since they are sometimes mixed with our own passions, they are the occasion of loud sobbing; and I have heard some persons say they experience a tightening in the chest and even external bodily movements that they cannot restrain. The force of these passions can cause nosebleeds and other things just as painful. I don't know how to explain anything about these experiences, because I haven't had any. But they must nonetheless be consoling, for, as I'm saying, the whole experience ends in the desire to please God and enjoy His Majesty's company.

The experiences that I call spiritual delight in God, that I termed elsewhere the prayer of quiet, are of a very different kind, as those of you who by the mercy of God have experienced them will know. Let's consider, for a better understanding, that we see two founts with two water troughs. (For I don't find anything more appropriate to explain some spiritual experiences than water; and this is because I know little and have no helpful cleverness of mind and am so fond of this element that I have observed it more attentively than other things. In all the things that so great and wise a God has created there must be many beneficial secrets, and those who understand them do benefit, although I believe that in each little thing created by God there is more than what is understood, even if it is a little ant.)

These two troughs are filled with water in different ways: with one, the water comes from far away through many aqueducts and the use of much ingenuity; with the other, the source of the water is right there, and the trough fills without any noise. If the spring is abundant, as is this one we are speaking about, the water overflows once the trough is filled, forming a large stream. There is no need of any skill, nor does the building of aqueducts have to continue; but water is always flowing from the spring.

The water coming from the aqueducts is comparable, in my opinion, to the consolations I mentioned that are drawn from meditation. For we obtain them through thoughts, assisting ourselves, using creatures to help our meditation, and tiring the intellect. Since, in the end, the consolation comes through our own efforts, noise is made when there has to be some replenishing of the benefits the consolation causes in the soul, as has been said.

With this other fount, the water comes from its own source, which is God. And since His Majesty desires to do so—when he is pleased to grant some supernatural favor—he produces this delight with the greatest peace and quiet and sweetness in the very interior part of ourselves. I don't know from where or how, nor is that happiness and delight experienced as are earthly consolations in the heart. I mean there is no similarity at the beginning, for afterward the delight fills everything; this water overflows through all the dwelling places and faculties until reaching the body. That is why I said that it begins in God and ends in ourselves. For, certainly, as anyone who may have experienced it will see, the whole exterior man enjoys this spiritual delight and sweetness.

I was now thinking, while writing this, that the verse mentioned above, *Dilatasti cor meum*, says the heart was expanded [Ps. 119:32]. I don't think the experience is something, as I say, that rises from the heart, but from another part still more interior, as from something deep. I think this must be the center of the soul, as I later came to understand and will mention at the end. For certainly I see secrets within ourselves that have often caused me to marvel. And how many more there must be! O my Lord and my God, how great are your grandeurs! We go about here below like foolish little shepherds, for while it seems that we are getting some knowledge of you, it must amount to no more than nothing; for even in our own selves there are great secrets that we don't understand. I say "no more than nothing" because I'm comparing it to the many, many secrets that are in you, not because the grandeurs we see in you are not extraordinary; and that includes those we can attain knowledge of through your works.

To return to the verse, what I think is helpful in it for explaining this matter is the idea of expansion. It seems that since that heavenly water begins to rise from this spring I'm mentioning that is deep within us, it swells and expands our whole interior being, producing ineffable blessings; nor does the soul even understand what is given to it there. It perceives a fragrance, let us say for now, as though there were in that interior depth a brazier giving off sweet-smelling perfumes. No light is seen, nor is the place seen where the brazier is; but the warmth and the fragrant fumes spread through the entire soul and even often enough, as I have said, the body shares in them. See now that you understand me; no heat is felt, nor is there the scent of any perfume, for the experience is more delicate than an experience of these things; but I use the examples only so as to explain it to you. And let persons who have not experienced these things understand that truthfully they do happen and are felt in this way, and the soul understands them in a manner clearer than is my explanation right now. This spiritual delight is not something that can be imagined, because however diligent our efforts, we cannot acquire it. The very experience of it makes us realize that it is not of the same metal as we ourselves, but fashioned from the purest gold of the divine wisdom. Here, in my opinion, the faculties are not united, but absorbed and looking as though in wonder at what they see.

It's possible that in dealing with these interior matters I might contradict something of what I said elsewhere. That's no surprise, because, in the almost fifteen years since I wrote it, the Lord may perhaps have given me clearer understanding in these matters than I had before. Now, as then, I could be completely mistaken—but I would not lie, because by God's mercy I'd rather suffer a thousand deaths. I speak of what I understand.

It seems clear to me that the will must in some way be united with God's will. But it is in the effects and deeds following afterward that one discerns the true value of prayer; there is no better crucible for testing prayer. It is quite a great favor from our Lord if the person receiving the favor recognizes it, and a very great one if he doesn't turn back.

You will at once desire, my daughters, to obtain this prayer; and you are right, for, as I have said, the soul will never understand the favors the Lord is granting there or the love with which he is drawing it nearer to himself. It is good to try to understand how we can obtain such a favor; so I am going to tell you what I have understood about this.

Let's leave aside the times when our Lord is pleased to grant it because he wants to and for no other reason. He knows why; we don't have to meddle in this. After you have done what should be done by those in the previous dwelling places: humility! humility! By this means the Lord allows himself to be conquered with regard to anything we want from him. The first sign for seeing whether or not you have humility is that you do not think you deserve these favors and spiritual delights from the Lord or that you will receive them in your lifetime.

You will ask me how, then, one can obtain them without seeking them. I answer that for the following reasons there is no better way than the one I mentioned, of not striving for them. First, because the initial thing necessary for such favors is to love God without self-interest. Second, because there is a slight lack of humility in thinking that for our miserable services something so great can be obtained. Third, because the authentic preparation for these favors on the part of those of us who, after all, have offended him is the desire to suffer and imitate the Lord rather than to have spiritual delights. Fourth, because His Majesty is not obliged to give them to us as he is to give us glory if we keep his commandments. (Without these favors we can be saved, and he knows better than we ourselves what is fitting for us and who of us truly love him. This is certain, I know. And I know persons who walk by the path of love as they ought to walk, that is, only so as to serve their Christ crucified; not only do these persons refuse to seek spiritual delights from him or to desire them, but they beseech him not to give them these favors during their life-time. This is true.) The fifth reason is that we would be laboring in vain; for since this water must not be drawn through aqueducts as was the previous water, we are little helped by tiring ourselves if the spring doesn't want to produce it. I mean that no matter how much we meditate or how much we try to squeeze something out and have tears, this water doesn't come in such a way. It is given only to whom God wills to give it and often when the soul is least thinking of it.

We belong to him, daughters. Let him do whatever he likes with us, bring us wherever he pleases. I really believe that whoever humbles himself and is detached (I mean in fact, because the detachment and humility must not be just in our thoughts—for they often deceive us—but complete) will receive the favor of this water from the Lord and many other favors that we don't know how to desire. May he be forever praised and blessed, amen.

Chapter 3

Deals with the prayer of recollection, which for the most part the Lord gives before the prayer just mentioned. Tells about its effects and about those that come from that spiritual delight, given by the Lord, that was discussed in the previous chapter.

The effects of this prayer are many. I shall mention some. But first, I want to mention another kind of prayer that almost always begins before this one. Since I have spoken of such a prayer elsewhere, I shall say little. It is a recollection that also seems to me to be supernatural because it doesn't involve being in the dark or closing the eyes, nor does it consist in any exterior thing, since without first wanting to do so, one does close one's eyes and desire solitude. It seems that without any contrivance the edifice is being built, by means of this recollection, for the prayer that was mentioned. The senses and exterior things seem to be losing their hold, because the soul is recovering what it had lost.

They say that the soul enters within itself and, at other times, that it rises above itself. With such terminology I wouldn't know how to clarify anything. This is what's wrong with me: that I think you will understand by my way of explaining, while perhaps I'm the only one who will understand myself. Let us suppose that these senses and faculties (for I have already mentioned that these powers are the people of this castle, which is the image I have taken for my explanation) have gone outside and have walked for days and years with strangers—enemies of the well-being of the castle. Having seen their perdition, they've already begun to approach the castle, even though they may not manage to remain inside because the habit of doing so is difficult to acquire. But still they are not traitors, and they walk in the environs of the castle. Once the great King, who is in the center dwelling place of this castle, sees their good will, he desires in his wonderful mercy to bring them back to him. Like a good shepherd, with a whistle so gentle that even they themselves almost fail to hear it, he makes them recognize his voice and stops them from going so far astray and brings them back to their dwelling place. And this shepherd's whistle has such power that they abandon the exterior things in which they were estranged from him and enter the castle.

I don't think I've ever explained it as clearly as I have now. When God grants the favor it is a great help to seek him within, where he is found more easily and in a way more beneficial to us than when sought in creatures, as St. Augustine says after having looked for him in many places. Don't think this recollection is acquired by the intellect striving to think about God within itself, or by the imagination imagining him within itself. Such efforts are good and an excellent kind of meditation because they are founded on a truth, which is that God is within us. But this isn't the prayer of recollection, because it is something each one can do—with the help of God, as should be understood of everything. But what I'm speaking of comes in a different way. Sometimes before one begins to think of God, these people are already inside the castle. I don't know in what way or how they heard their shepherd's whistle. It wasn't through the ears, because nothing is heard. But one noticeably senses a gentle drawing inward, as anyone who goes through this will observe, for I don't know how to make it clearer. It seems to me that I have read where it was compared to a hedgehog curling up or a turtle drawing into its shell. (The one who wrote this example must have understood the experience well.) But these creatures draw inward whenever they want. In the case of this recollection, it doesn't come when we want it, but when God wants to grant us the favor. I, for myself, hold that when His Majesty grants it, he does so to persons who are already beginning to despise the things of the world. I don't say that those in the married state do so in deed, for they cannot, but in desire; for he calls such persons especially so that they might be attentive to interior matters. So I believe that if we desire to make room for His Majesty, he will give not only this but more, and give it to those whom he begins to call to advance farther.

May whoever experiences this within himself praise God greatly, because it is indeed right to recognize the favor and give thanks, for doing so will dispose one for other, greater favors. And this recollection is a preparation for being able to listen, as is counseled in some books, so that the soul, instead of striving to engage in discourse, strives to remain attentive and aware of what the Lord is working in it. If His Majesty has not begun to absorb us, I cannot understand how the mind can be stopped. There's no way of doing so without bringing about more harm than good, although there has been a lengthy controversy on this matter among some spiritual persons. For my part I must confess my lack of humility, but those in favor of stopping the mind have never given me a reason for submitting to what they say. One of them tried to convince me with a certain book by the saintly Friar Peter of Alcántara—for I believe he is a saint—to whom I would submit because I know that he knew. And we read it together, and he says the same thing I do, although not in my words. But it is clear in what he says that love must be already awakened. It could be that I'm mistaken, but I have the following reasons.

First, in this work of the spirit the one who thinks less and has less desire to act does more. What we must do is to beg like the needy poor before a rich and great emperor, and then lower our eyes and wait with humility. When through his secret paths it seems we understand that he hears us, then it is good to be silent, since he has allowed us to remain near him; and it will not be wrong to avoid working with the intellect—if we can work with it, I mean. But if we don't yet know whether this King has heard or seen us, we mustn't become fools. The soul does become quite a fool when it tries to induce this prayer, and it is left much drier;

and the imagination perhaps becomes more restless through the effort made not to think of anything. But the Lord desires that we beseech him and call to mind that we are in his presence; he knows what is suitable for us. I cannot persuade myself to use human diligence in a matter in which it seems that His Majesty has placed a limit, and I want to leave the diligence to him. What he did not reserve to himself are many other efforts we can make with his help, such as penance, good deeds, and prayer—insofar as our wretchedness can do these things.

The second reason is that these interior works are all gentle and peaceful; doing something arduous would cause more harm than good. I call any force that we might want to use "something arduous"; for example, it would be arduous to hold one's breath. Leave the soul in God's hands, let him do whatever he wants with it, with the greatest disinterest about your own benefit as is possible and the greatest resignation to the will of God.

The third reason is that the very care used not to think of anything will perhaps rouse the mind to think very much.

The fourth is that what is most essential and pleasing to God is that we be mindful of his honor and glory and forget ourselves and our own profit and comfort and delight. How is a person forgetful of self if he is so careful not to stir or even to allow his intellect or desires to be stirred to a longing for the greater glory of God, or if he rests in what he already has? When His Majesty desires the intellect to stop, he occupies it in another way and gives it a light so far above what we can attain that it remains absorbed. Then, without knowing how, the intellect is much better instructed than it was through all the soul's efforts not to make use of it. Since God gave us our faculties that we might work with them and in this work they find their reward, there is no reason to charm them; we should let them perform their task until God appoints them to another, greater one.

What I understand to be most fitting for the soul the Lord has desired to put in this dwelling place is that which has been said. And without any effort or noise the soul should strive to cut down the rambling of the intellect—but not suspend either it or the mind; it is good to be aware of who God is and that one is in God's presence. If what it feels within itself absorbs it, well and good. But let it not strive to understand the nature of this recollection, for this recollection is given to the will. Let the soul enjoy it without any endeavors other than some loving words, for even though we may not try in this prayer to go without thinking of anything, I know that often the intellect will be suspended, even though for only a very brief moment.

But as I said elsewhere, the reason why in this kind of prayer, that is, the kind that is like the flowing spring in which the water does not come through aqueducts, the soul restrains itself or is restrained in its realization that it doesn't understand what it desires; and so the mind wanders from one extreme to the other, like a fool unable to rest in anything. (I am referring to the kind of prayer this dwelling place began with, for I have joined the prayer of recollection, which I should have mentioned first, with this one. The prayer of recollection is much less intense than the prayer of spiritual delight from God that I mentioned; but it is the beginning through which one goes to the other, for in the prayer of recollection meditation, or the work of the intellect, must not be set aside.) The will has such deep rest in its God that the clamor of the intellect is a terrible bother to it. There is no need to pay any attention to this clamor, for doing so would make the will lose much of what it enjoys. But one should let the intellect go and surrender oneself into the arms of love, for His Majesty will teach the soul what it must do at that point. Almost everything lies in finding oneself unworthy of so great a good and in being occupied with giving thanks.

In order to deal with the prayer of recollection I postponed mention of the effects or signs in souls to whom God, our Lord, gives this prayer of quiet. What an expansion or dilation of the soul is may be clearly understood from the example of a fount whose water doesn't overflow into a stream because the fount itself is constructed of such material that the more water there is flowing into it, the larger the trough becomes. So it seems is the case with this prayer and with many other marvels that God grants to the soul, for he enables and prepares it so that it can keep everything within itself. Hence this interior sweetness and expansion can be verified in the fact that the soul is not as tied down as it was before in things pertaining to the service of God, but has much more freedom. Thus, in not being constrained by the fear of hell (because although there is even greater fear of offending God, it loses servile fear here), this soul is left with great confidence that it will enjoy him. The fear it used to have of doing penance and losing its health has disappeared, and it now thinks it will be able to do all things in God [Phil. 4:13] and has greater desire for penance than previously. The fear it used to have of trials it now sees to be tempered. Its faith is more alive; it knows that if it suffers trials for God, His Majesty will give it the grace to suffer them with patience. Sometimes it even desires them because there also remains a strong will to do something for God. Since its knowledge of God's grandeur grows, it considers itself to be more miserable. Because it has already experienced spiritual delight from God, it sees that worldly delights are like filth. It finds itself withdrawing from them little by little, and it is more master of itself for so doing. In sum, there is an improvement in all the virtues. It will continue to grow, if it doesn't turn back now to offending God; because if it does, then everything will be lost, however high on the summit the soul may be. Nor should it be understood that if God grants this favor once or twice to a soul, all these good effects will be caused. It must persevere in receiving them, for in this perseverance lies all our good.

One strong warning I give to whoever finds himself in this state is that he guard very carefully against placing himself in the occasion of offending God. In this prayer the soul is not yet grown, but is like a suckling child. If it turns away from its mother's breasts, what can be expected for it but death? I am very much afraid that this will happen to anyone to whom God has granted this favor and who withdraws from prayer—unless he does so for a particularly special reason—or if he doesn't return quickly to prayer, for he will go from bad to worse. I know there is a great deal to fear in this matter. And I know some persons for whom I have felt quite sorry—and I've seen what I'm speaking about—because they have turned away from one who with so much love wanted to be their friend and proved it by deeds. I advise them so strongly not to place themselves in the occasions of sin, because the devil tries much harder for a soul of this kind than for very many to whom the Lord does not grant these favors. For such a soul can be of great benefit to God's church and do a great deal of harm to the devil by getting others to follow it. And even though the devil may have no other reason than to see who it is to whom His Majesty shows particular love, that's sufficient for him to wear himself out trying to lead the soul to perdition. So these souls suffer much combat, and if they go astray, they do so much more than others.

You, sisters, are free of dangers, from what we can know. From pride and vainglory may God deliver you. If the devil should counterfeit God's favors, this will be known by the fact that these good effects are not caused, but just the opposite.

There is one danger I want to warn you about (although I may have mentioned it elsewhere) into which I have seen persons of prayer fall, especially women, for, since we are weaker, there is more occasion for what I'm about to say. It is that some have a weak constitution because of a great amount of penance, prayer, and keeping vigil, and even without these, in receiving some favor, their nature is overcome. Since they feel some consolation interiorly and a languishing and weakness exteriorly, they think they are experiencing a spiritual sleep (which is a prayer a little more intense than the prayer of quiet), and they let themselves become absorbed. The more they allow this, the more absorbed they become, because their nature is further weakened, and they fancy that they are being carried away in rapture. I call it being carried away in foolishness, because it amounts to nothing more than wasting time and wearing down one's health. These persons feel nothing through their senses, nor do they feel anything concerning God. One person happened to remain eight hours in this state. By sleeping and eating and avoiding so much penance, this person got rid of the stupor, for there was someone who understood her. She had misled both her confessor and other persons, as well as herself—for she hadn't intended to deceive. I truly believe that the devil was trying to gain ground, and in this instance indeed he was beginning to gain no small amount.

It must be understood that, when something is truly from God, there is no languishing in the soul, even though there may be interior and exterior languishing. The soul experiences deep feelings when it sees itself close to God. Nor does the experience last so long, but for a very short while—although one becomes absorbed again. In such prayer, if the cause of it is not weakness, as I said, the body is not worn down, nor is any external feeling produced. For this reason let them take the advice that, when they feel this languishing in themselves, they tell the prioress and distract themselves from it insofar as they can. The prioress should make them give up so many hours for prayer so that they have only a very few and try to get them to sleep and eat well until their natural strength begins to return, if it has been lost through a lack of food and sleep. If a sister's nature is so weak that this is not enough, may she believe me that God does not want her to practice anything but the active life, which also must be practiced in monasteries. They should let her get busy with different duties, and always take care that she not have a great deal of solitude, for she would lose her health completely. It will be quite a mortification for her; in how she bears this absence is the way the Lord wants to test her love for him. And he will be pleased to give her strength back after some time. If he doesn't, she will gain through vocal prayer and through obedience and will merit what she would have merited otherwise, and perhaps more.

There could also be some persons with such weak heads and imaginations—and I have known some—to whom it seems that everything they think about they see. This is very dangerous. Because I shall perhaps treat it farther on, I'll say no more here. I have greatly enlarged on this dwelling place, because it is the one that more souls enter. Since it is, and since the natural and the supernatural are joined in it, the devil can do more harm. In those dwelling places still to be spoken of, the Lord doesn't give him so much leeway. May His Majesty be forever praised, amen.

THE FIFTH
DWELLING PLACES

Chapter 1

*Begins to deal with how the soul is united to God in
prayer. Tells how one discerns whether there is any illusion.*

O sisters, how can I explain the riches and treasures and delights
found in the fifth dwelling places? I believe it would be better not
to say anything about these remaining rooms, for there is no way
of learning how to speak of them; neither is the intellect capable of
understanding them, nor can comparisons help in explaining
them; earthly things are too coarse for such a purpose.

Send light from heaven, my Lord, that I might be able to
enlighten these your servants—for you have been pleased that
some of them ordinarily enjoy these delights—so that they may
not be deceived by the devil transforming himself into an angel
of light [2 Cor. 11:14]. For all their desires are directed toward
pleasing you.

And although I have said "some," there are indeed only a few
who fail to enter this dwelling place of which I shall now speak.
There are various degrees, and for that reason I say that most enter
these places. But I believe that only a few will experience some of
the things that I will say are in this room. Yet even if souls do no
more than reach the door, God is being very merciful to them;
although many are called, few are chosen [Matt. 22:14]. So I say
now that all of us who wear this holy habit of Carmel are called to
prayer and contemplation. This call explains our origin; we are the
descendants of men who felt this call, of those holy fathers on

Mount Carmel who in such great solitude and contempt for the world sought this treasure, this precious pearl of contemplation that we are speaking about. Yet few of us dispose ourselves that the Lord may communicate it to us. In exterior matters we are proceeding well, so that we will reach what is necessary; but in the practice of the virtues that are necessary for arriving at this point we need very, very much and cannot be careless in either small things or great. So, my sisters, since in some way we can enjoy heaven on earth, be brave in begging the Lord to give us his grace in such a way that nothing will be lacking through our own fault; that he show us the way and strengthen the soul that it may dig until it finds this hidden treasure [Matt. 13:44]. The truth is that the treasure lies within our very selves. This is what I would like to know how to explain, if the Lord would enable me to do so.

I said "strengthen the soul" so that you will understand that bodily strength is not necessary for those to whom God does not give it. He doesn't make it impossible for anyone to buy his riches. He is content if each one gives what he has. Blessed be so great a God. But reflect, daughters, that he doesn't want you to hold on to anything, for if you avoid doing so you will be able to enjoy the favors we are speaking of. Whether you have little or much, he wants everything for himself; and in conformity with what you know you have given, you will receive greater or lesser favors. There is no better proof for recognizing whether our prayer has reached union or not. Don't think this union is some kind of dreamy state like the one I mentioned before. I say "dreamy state" because it seems that the soul is as though asleep; yet neither does it really think it is asleep, nor does it feel awake. There is no need here to use any technique to suspend the mind, since all the faculties are asleep in this state— and truly asleep—to the things of the world and to ourselves. As a matter of fact, during the time that the union lasts, the soul is left as though without its senses, for it has no power to think even if it wants to. In loving, if it does love, it doesn't understand how or what it is it loves or what it would want. In sum, it is like one who in every respect has died to the world, so as to live more completely in God. Thus the death is a delightful one, an uprooting from the soul of all the operations the latter can have while being in the body. The death is a delightful one because in truth it seems that, in order to dwell more perfectly in God, the soul is so separated from the body that I don't even know if it has life enough to breathe. (I was just now thinking about this, and it seems to me that it doesn't—at least if it does breathe, it is unaware that it is doing so.) Nonetheless, its whole intellect would want to be occupied in understanding something of what is felt. And since the soul does not have the energy to attain to this, it is so stunned that, even if it is not completely lost, neither a hand nor a foot stirs, as we say here below when a person is in such a swoon that we think he is dead.

O secrets of God! I would never tire of trying to explain them if I thought I could in some way manage to do so; thus I will say a thousand foolish things in order that I might at times succeed and that we might give great praise to the Lord.

I said that this union was not some kind of dreamy state,

because even if the experience in the dwelling place that was mentioned is abundant, the soul remains doubtful that it was union. It doubts whether it imagined the experience; whether it was asleep; whether the experience was given by God; or whether the devil transformed himself into an angel of light. It is left with a thousand suspicions. That it has them is good, for, as I have said, even our own nature can sometimes deceive us in that dwelling place. Though there is not so much room for poisonous things to enter, some tiny lizards do enter; since these lizards have slender heads, they can poke their heads in anywhere. And even though they do no harm, especially if one pays no attention to them, as I said, they are often a bother, since they are little thoughts proceeding from the imagination and from what I mentioned. But however slender they may be, these little lizards cannot enter this fifth dwelling place; for there is neither imagination, nor memory, nor intellect that can impede this good. And I would dare say that, if the prayer is truly union with God, the devil cannot even enter or do any damage. His Majesty is so joined and united with the essence of the soul that the devil will not dare approach, nor will he even know about this secret. And this is obvious. Since, as they say, he doesn't know our mind, he will have less knowledge of something so secret; for God doesn't even entrust this to our own mind. Oh, what a great good, a state in which this accursed one does us no harm! Thus the soul is left with such wonderful blessings, because God works within it without anyone's disturbing him, not even ourselves. What will he not give, who is so fond of giving and who can give all that he wants?

It seems that I have left you confused by saying "if it is union" and that there are other unions. And, indeed, how true it is that there are! Even though these unions regard vain things, the devil will use such things to transport us when they are greatly loved. But he doesn't do so in the way God does, or with the delight and satisfaction of soul, or with the peace and joy. This union is above all earthly joys, above all delights, above all consolations, and still more than that. It doesn't matter where those spiritual or earthly joys come from, for the feeling is very different, as you will have experienced. I once said that the difference is like that between feeling something on the rough outer covering of the body or in the marrow of the bones. And that was right on the mark, for I don't know how to say it better.

It seems to me that you're still not satisfied, for you will think you can be mistaken and that these interior things are something difficult to examine. What was said will be sufficient for anyone who has experienced union. Yet because the difference between union and the previous experience is great, I want to mention a clear sign by which you will be sure against error or doubts about whether the union is from God. His Majesty has brought it to my memory today, and in my opinion it is the sure sign. In difficult matters, even though it seems to me that I understand and that I speak the truth, I always use the expression "it seems to me." For if I am mistaken, I'm very much prepared to believe what those who have a great deal of learning say. Even though they have not experienced these things, very learned men have a certain I don't know what; for since God destines them to give

light to his church, he enlightens them that they might acknowl-
edge a truth when presented with it. And if they do not live a
dissipated life, but are God's servants, they are never surprised by
his grandeurs; they have come to understand well that he can do
ever more and more. And, finally, even though some things are
not so well explained, these learned men will find others in their
books through which they will see that these things could take
place.

I have had a great deal of experience with learned men, and
have also had experience with half-learned, fearful ones; these
latter cost me dearly. At least I think that anyone who refuses to
believe that God can do much more or that he has considered and
continues to consider it good sometimes to communicate favors
to his creatures has indeed closed the door to receiving them.
Therefore, sisters, let this never happen to you, but believe that
God can do far more and don't turn your attention to whether
the ones to whom he grants his favors are good or bad; for His
Majesty knows this, as I have told you. There is no reason for us to
meddle in the matter, but with humility and simplicity of heart
we should serve and praise him for his works and marvels.

Now then, to return to the sign that I say is the true one: you
now see that God has made this soul a fool with regard to all, so
as better to impress upon it true wisdom. For during the time of
this union it neither sees, nor hears, nor understands, because the
union is always short and seems to the soul even much shorter
than it probably is. God so places himself in the interior of that
soul that, when it returns to itself, it can in no way doubt that it

was in God and God was in it. This truth remains with it so firmly that, even though years go by without God's granting that favor again, the soul can neither forget nor doubt that it was in God and God was in it. This is what matters now, for I shall speak of the effects of this prayer afterward.

Now, you will ask me, how did the soul see this truth or understand if it didn't see or understand anything? I don't say that it then saw the truth, but that afterward it sees the truth clearly, not because of a vision, but because of a certitude remaining in the soul that only God can place there. I know a person who hadn't learned that God was in all things by presence, power, and essence, and through a favor of this kind that God granted her she came to believe it. After asking a half-learned man of the kind I mentioned—he knew as little as she had known before God enlightened her—she was told that God was present only by grace. Such was her own conviction that even after this she didn't believe him and asked others who told her the truth, with which she was greatly consoled.

Don't be mistaken by thinking that this certitude has to do with a corporal form, as in the case of the bodily presence of our Lord Jesus Christ in the Most Blessed Sacrament even though we do not see him. Here the matter isn't like that; it concerns only the divinity. How, then, is it that what we do not see leaves this certitude? I don't know; these are his works. But I do know I speak the truth. And I would say that whoever does not receive this certitude does not experience union of the whole soul with God, but union of some faculty, or that he experiences one of the many other kinds of favors God grants souls. In regard to all these favors we have to give up looking for reasons to see how they've come about. Since our intellect cannot understand this union, why do we have to make this effort? It's enough for us to see that he who is the cause of it is almighty. Since we have no part at all to play in bringing it about, no matter how much effort we put forth, but it is God who does so, let us not desire the capacity to understand this union.

Now I recall, in saying that we have no part to play, what you have heard the bride say in the Song of Songs: "He brought me into the wine cellar" (or "placed me there," I believe it says) [Song of Sol. 2:4]. And it doesn't say that she went. And she says also that she went looking about in every part of the city for her beloved [Song of Sol. 3:2]. I understand this union to be the wine cellar where the Lord wishes to place us when he desires and as he desires. But however great the effort we make to do so, we cannot enter. His Majesty must place us there and enter himself into the center of our soul. And that he may show his marvels more clearly, he doesn't want our will to have any part to play, for it has been entirely surrendered to him. Neither does he want the door of the faculties and of the senses to be opened, for they are all asleep. But he wants to enter the center of the soul without going through any door, as he entered the place where his disciples were when he said *pax vobis* ["Peace to you," John 20:19] or as he left the tomb without lifting away the stone. Farther on you will see in the last dwelling place how His Majesty desires that the soul enjoy him in its own center even much more than here.

O daughters, how much we shall see if we don't want to have

anything more to do with our own lowliness and misery and if
we understand that we are unworthy of being servants of a Lord
who is so great we cannot comprehend his wonders! May he be
forever praised, amen.

Chapter 2

Continues on the same topic. Explains the prayer
of union through an exquisite comparison. Tells about the
effects it leaves in the soul. The chapter
is very important.

It will seem to you that everything has already been said about
what there is to see in this dwelling place. Yet a lot is missing, for,
as I said, there are various degrees of intensity. With regard to the
nature of union, I don't believe I'd know how to say anything
more. But when souls to whom God grants these favors prepare
themselves, there are many things to say about the Lord's work in
them. I shall speak of some of these and tell about the state the
soul is left in. To explain things better, I want to use a helpful
comparison; it is good for making us see how, even though we
can do nothing in this work done by the Lord, we can do much
by disposing ourselves so that His Majesty may grant us this favor.

You must have already heard about his marvels manifested in the
way silk originates, for only he could have invented something like
that. The silkworms come from seeds about the size of little grains
of pepper. (I have never seen this but have heard of it, and so if

something in the explanation gets distorted, it won't be my fault.)
When the warm weather comes and the leaves begin to appear on
the mulberry tree, the seeds start to live, for they are dead until then.
The worms nourish themselves on the mulberry leaves until, having
grown to full size, they settle on some twigs. There, with their little
mouths, they themselves go about spinning the silk and making
some very thick little cocoons in which they enclose themselves.
The silkworm, which is fat and ugly, then dies, and a little white
butterfly, which is very pretty, comes forth from the cocoon. Now,
if this were not seen but recounted to us as having happened in
other times, who would believe it? Or what reasonings could make
us conclude that a thing as nonrational as a worm or a bee could be
so diligent in working for our benefit and with so much industri-
ousness? And the poor little worm loses its life in the challenge. This
is enough, sisters, for a period of meditation even though I may say
no more to you; in it you can consider the wonders and the wisdom
of our God. Well, now, what would happen if we knew the property
of every created thing? It is very beneficial for us to busy ourselves
thinking of these grandeurs and delighting in being brides of a King
so wise and powerful.

Let's return to what I was saying. This silkworm, then, starts to
live when, by the heat of the Holy Spirit, it begins to benefit
through the general help given to us all by God and through the
remedies left by him to his church, by going to confession, reading good books, and hearing sermons, which are the remedies
that a soul, dead in its carelessness and sins and placed in the
midst of occasions, can make use of. It then begins to live and to

sustain itself by these things, and by good meditations, until it is grown. Its being grown is what is relevant to what I'm saying, for these other things have little importance here.

Well, once this silkworm is grown—in the beginning I dealt with its growth—it begins to spin the silk and build the house wherein it will die. I would like to point out here that this house is Christ. Somewhere, it seems to me, I have read or heard that our life is hidden in Christ or in God (both are the same) or that our life is Christ [Col. 3:3–4]. Whether the quotation is exact or not doesn't matter for what I intend.

Well, see here, daughters, what we can do through the help of God: His Majesty himself, as he does in this prayer of union, becomes the dwelling place we build for ourselves. It seems I'm saying that we can build up God and take him away, since I say that he is the dwelling place and we ourselves can build it so as to place ourselves in it. And, indeed, we can! Not that we can take God away or build him up, but we can take away from ourselves and build up, as do these little silkworms. For we will not have finished doing all that we can in this work when, to the little we do, which is nothing, God will unite himself, with his greatness, and give it such high value that the Lord himself will become the reward of this work. Thus, since it was he who paid the highest price, His Majesty wants to join our little labors with the great ones he suffered, so that all the work may become one.

Therefore, courage, my daughters! Let's be quick to do this work and weave this little cocoon by taking away our self-love and self-will, our attachment to any earthly thing, and by per-

forming deeds of penance, prayer, mortification, obedience, and
of all the other things you know. Would to heaven that we would
do what we know we must; and we are instructed about what we
must do. Let it die; let this silkworm die, as it does in completing
what it was created to do! And you will see how we see God, as
well as ourselves placed inside his grandeur, as is this little silkworm within its cocoon. Keep in mind that I say "see God" in the
sense of what I mentioned concerning that which is felt in this
kind of union.

Now then, let's see what this silkworm does, for that's the reason I've said everything else. When the soul is, in this prayer,
truly dead to the world, a little white butterfly comes forth. Oh
greatness of God! How transformed the soul is when it comes
out of this prayer after having been placed within the greatness
of God and so closely joined with him for a little while—in my
opinion the union never lasts for as much as a half hour. Truly, I
tell you that the soul doesn't recognize itself. Look at the difference there is between an ugly worm and a little white butterfly;
that's what the difference is here. The soul doesn't know how it
could have merited so much good—from where this good may
have come, I mean, for it well knows that it doesn't merit this
blessing. It sees within itself a desire to praise the Lord; it would
want to dissolve and die a thousand deaths for him. It soon
begins to experience a desire to suffer great trials without its
being able to do otherwise. There are the strongest desires for
penance, for solitude, and that all might know God; and great
pain comes to it when it sees that he is offended. I shall treat

these things more particularly in the next dwelling place; although what is in this dwelling place and the next are almost identical, the force of the effects is very different. As I have said, if after God brings a soul here it makes the effort to advance, it will see great things.

Oh, now, to see the restlessness of this little butterfly, even though it has never been quieter and calmer in its life, is something to praise God for! And the difficulty is that it doesn't know where to alight and rest. Since it has experienced such wonderful rest, all that it sees on earth displeases it, especially if God gives it this wine often. Almost each time it gains new treasures. It no longer has any esteem for the works it did while a worm, which was to weave the cocoon little by little; it now has wings. How can it be happy walking step by step when it can fly? On account of its desires, everything it can do for God becomes little in its own eyes. It doesn't wonder as much at what the saints suffered, now that it understands through experience how the Lord helps and transforms a soul, for it doesn't recognize itself or its image. The weakness it previously seemed to have with regard to doing penance it now finds is its strength. Its attachment to relatives or friends or wealth (for neither its actions, nor its determination, nor its desire to withdraw were enough; rather, in its opinion, it was more attached to everything) is now so looked upon that it grieves when obliged to do what is necessary in this regard so as not to offend God. Everything wearies it, for it has learned through experience that creatures cannot give it true rest.

It seems I have been lengthy, but I could say much more; and whoever has received this favor from God will see that I've been brief. So there is no reason to be surprised that this little butterfly seeks rest again, since it feels estranged from earthly things. Well, then, where will the poor little thing go? It can't return to where it came from; as was said, we are powerless, however much we do, to bring about this favor until God is again pleased to grant it. O Lord, what new trials begin for this soul! Who would say such a thing after a favor so sublime? Briefly, in one way or another there must be a cross while we live, and with respect to anyone who says that after he arrived here he always enjoyed rest and delight, I would say that he never arrived, but that perhaps he had experienced some spiritual delight—if he had entered into the previous dwelling places and his experiences had been helped along by natural weakness or perhaps even by the devil, who gives him peace so as afterward to wage much greater war against him.

I don't mean to say that those who arrive here do not have peace; they do have it, and it is very deep. For the trials themselves are so valuable and have such good roots that, although very severe, they give rise to peace and happiness. From the very unhappiness caused by worldly things arises the ever so painful desire to leave this world. Any relief the soul has comes from the thought that God wants it to be living in this exile; yet even this is not enough, because in spite of all these benefits it is not entirely surrendered to God's will, as will be seen farther on—although it doesn't fail to conform itself. But it conforms with a great feeling that it can do no more because no more has been given it, and with many tears. Every time it is in prayer this regret is its pain. In some way perhaps the sorrow proceeds from the deep pain it feels at seeing that God is offended and little esteemed in this world and that many souls are lost, heretics as well as Moors; although those that grieve it most are Christians. Even though it sees that God's mercy is great—for, however wicked their lives, these Christians can make amends and be saved—it fears that many are being condemned.

O greatness of God! A few years ago—and even perhaps days—this soul wasn't mindful of anything but itself. Who has placed it in the midst of such painful concerns? Even were we to meditate for many years, we wouldn't be able to feel them as painfully as does this soul now. Well, God help me, wouldn't it be enough if, for many days and years, I strove to think about the tremendous evil of an offense against God and that those souls who are condemned are his children and my brothers and about the dangers in which we live and how good it is for us to leave this miserable life? Not at all, daughters; the grief that is felt here is not like that of this world. We can, with God's favor, feel the grief that comes from thinking about these things a great deal, but such grief doesn't reach the intimate depths of our being as does the pain suffered in this state, for it seems that the pain breaks and grinds the soul into pieces, without the soul's striving for it or even at times wanting it. Well, what is this pain? Where does it come from? I shall tell you.

Haven't you heard it said of the bride—for I have already mentioned it elsewhere here, but not in this sense—that God brought her into the inner wine cellar and put charity in order within her

THE FIFTH DWELLING PLACES 65

[Song of Sol. 2:4]? Well, that is what I mean. Since that soul now surrenders itself into his hands and its great love makes it so surrendered that it neither knows nor wants anything more than what he wants with her (for God will never, in my judgment, grant this favor save to a soul that he takes for his own), he desires that, without its understanding how, it may go forth from this union impressed with his seal. For, indeed, the soul does no more in this union than does the wax when another impresses a seal on it. The wax doesn't impress the seal upon itself; it is only disposed—I mean, by being soft. And even in order to be disposed it doesn't soften itself, but remains still and gives its consent. O goodness of God, everything must be at a cost to you! All you want is our will and that there be no impediment in the wax.

Well, now, you see here, sisters, what our God does in this union so that this soul may recognize itself as his own. He gives from what he has, which is what his Son had in this life. He cannot grant us a higher favor. Who could have had a greater desire to leave this life? And so His Majesty said at the Last Supper: "I have earnestly desired" [Luke 22:15].

Well, then, how is it, Lord, that you weren't thinking of the laborious death you were about to suffer, so painful and frightful? You answer: "No, my great love and the desire I have that souls be saved are incomparably more important than these sufferings; and the very greatest sorrows that I have suffered and do suffer, after being in the world, are not enough to be considered anything at all in comparison with this love and desire to save souls."

This is true, for I have often reflected on the matter. I know the torment a certain soul of my acquaintance suffers and has suffered at seeing our Lord offended. The pain is so unbearable that she desires to die much more than to suffer it. If a soul with so little charity when compared with Christ's—for its charity could be then considered almost nonexistent—felt this torment to be so unbearable, what must have been the feeling of our Lord Jesus Christ? And what kind of life must he have suffered, since all things were present to him and he was always witnessing the serious offenses committed against his Father? I believe without a doubt that these sufferings were much greater than were those of his most sacred Passion. At the time of his Passion he already saw an end to these trials and, with this awareness as well as the happiness of seeing a remedy for us in his death and of showing us the love he had for his Father in suffering so much for him, he tempered his sorrows. These sorrows are also tempered here below by those who with the strength that comes from love perform great penances, for they almost don't feel them; rather, they would want to do more and more—and everything they do seems little to them. Well, what must it have been for His Majesty to find himself with so excellent an occasion for showing his Father how completely obedient he was to him, and with love for his neighbor? Oh great delight, to suffer in doing the will of God! But I consider it so difficult to see the many offenses committed so continually against His Majesty and the many souls going to hell that I believe only one day of that pain would have been sufficient to end many lives; how much more one life, if he had been no more than man.

THE SIXTH
DWELLING PLACES

Chapter 1

Discusses how greater trials come when the Lord begins to grant greater favors. Mentions some and how those who are now in this dwelling place conduct themselves. This chapter is good for souls undergoing interior trials.

Well, then, let us, with the help of the Holy Spirit, speak of the sixth dwelling places, where the soul is now wounded with love for its Spouse and strives for more opportunities to be alone and, in conformity with its state, to rid itself of everything that can be an obstacle to this solitude.

That meeting left such an impression that the soul's whole desire is to enjoy it again. I have already said that in this prayer nothing is seen in a way that can be called seeing, nor is anything seen with the imagination. I use the term "meeting" because of the comparison I made. Now the soul is fully determined to take no other spouse. But the Spouse does not look at the soul's great desires that the betrothal take place, for he still wants it to desire this more, and he wants the betrothal to take place at a cost; it is the greatest of blessings. And although everything is small when it comes to paying for this exceptional benefit, I tell you, daughters, that for the soul to endure such delay, it needs to have that token or pledge of betrothal that it now has. O God help me, what interior and exterior trials the soul suffers before entering the seventh dwelling place!

Indeed, sometimes I reflect and fear that if a soul knew beforehand, its natural weakness would find it most difficult to have the determination to suffer and pass through these trials, no matter what blessings were represented to it—unless it had arrived at the seventh dwelling place. For once it has arrived there, the soul fears nothing and is absolutely determined to overcome every obstacle for God. And the reason is that it is always so closely joined to His Majesty that from this union comes its fortitude. I believe it will be well to recount some of those trials that I know one will certainly undergo. Perhaps not all souls will be led along this path, although I doubt very much that those persons who sometimes enjoy so truly the things of heaven will live free of earthly trials that come in one way or another.

Although I hadn't intended to treat these, I thought doing so would bring great consolation to some soul going through them, for it would learn that these trials take place in souls to whom God grants similar favors; for, truly, when one is suffering the trials, it then seems that everything is lost. I will not deal with them according to the order in which they happen, but as they come to mind. And I want to begin with the smallest trials. There is an outcry by persons a sister is dealing with and even by those she does not deal with and who, it seems to her, would never even think of her, gossip like the following: "She's trying to make out she's a saint; she goes to extremes to deceive the world and bring others to ruin; there are other, better Christians who don't put on all this outward show." (And it's worth noting that she is not putting on any outward show, but just striving to fulfill well her state in life.) Those she considered her friends turn away from her, and they are the ones who take the largest and most painful bite at her: "That soul has gone astray and is clearly mistaken; these are things of the devil; she will turn out like this person or that other who went astray, and will bring about a decline in virtue; she has deceived her confessors" (and they go to these confessors, telling them so, giving them examples of what happened to some that were lost in this way); a thousand kinds of ridicule and sayings like the above.

I know a person who had great fear that there would be no one who would hear her confession because of such gossip—so much gossip that there's no reason to go into it all here. And what is worse, these things do not pass quickly, but go on throughout the person's whole life, including the advice to others to avoid any dealings with such persons.

You will tell me that there are also those who will speak well of that soul. O daughters, how few there are who believe in such favors in comparison with the many who denigrate them! Moreover, praise is just another trial greater than those mentioned! Since the soul sees clearly that, if it has anything good, this is given by God and is by no means its own—for just previously it saw itself to be very poor and surrounded by great sins—praise is an intolerable burden to it, at least in the beginning. Later on, for certain reasons, praise is not so intolerable. First, because experience makes the soul see clearly that people are as quick to say good things as bad, and so it pays no more attention to the good things than to the bad. Second, because it has been more enlightened by the Lord that no good thing comes from itself but is given by His Majesty; and it turns to praise God, forgetful that it has had any part to play, just as if it had seen the gift in another person. Third, if it sees that some souls have benefited from seeing the favors God grants it, it thinks that His Majesty used this means, of its being falsely esteemed as good, so that some blessings might come to those souls. Fourth, since it looks after the honor and glory of God more than its own, the temptation, which came in the beginning, that these praises will destroy it is removed; little does dishonor matter to it if in exchange God might perhaps thereby just once be praised—afterward, let whatever comes come.

These reasons and others mitigate the great pain these praises cause, although some pain is almost always felt, except when one is paying hardly any attention. But it is an incomparably greater trial to see oneself publicly considered as good without reason than the trials mentioned. And when the soul reaches the stage at which it pays little attention to praise, it pays much less to disapproval; on the contrary, it rejoices in this and finds it a very sweet music. This is an amazing truth. Blame does not intimidate the soul, but strengthens it. Experience has already taught it the wonderful gain that comes through this path. It feels that those who persecute it do not offend God; rather, that His Majesty permits persecution for the benefit of the soul. And since it clearly experiences the benefits of persecution, it acquires a special and very tender love for its persecutors. It seems to it that they are greater friends and more advantageous than those who speak well of it.

The Lord is wont also to send it the severest illnesses. This is a much greater trial, especially when the pains are acute. For, in some way, if these pains are severe, the trial is, it seems to me, the greatest on earth—I mean, the greatest exterior trial, however many the other pains. I say "if the pains are severe," because they then afflict the soul interiorly and exteriorly in such a way that it doesn't know what to do with itself. It would willingly accept at once any martyrdom rather than these sharp pains, although they do not last long in this extreme form. After all, God gives no more than what can be endured; and His Majesty gives patience first. But other great sufferings and illnesses of many kinds are the usual thing.

I know a person who cannot truthfully say that, from the time the Lord began forty years ago to grant the favor that was mentioned, she spent even one day without pains and other kinds of suffering (from lack of bodily health, I mean) and other great trials. It's true that she had been very wretched and that everything seemed small to her in comparison with the hell she deserved. Others, who have not offended our Lord so much, will be led by another path. But I would always choose the path of suffering, if only to imitate our Lord Jesus Christ, if there were no other gains, especially since there are always so many other things to gain.

Oh, were we to treat interior sufferings, these others would seem small if the interior ones could be clearly explained; but it is impossible to explain the way in which they come to pass.

Let us begin with the torment one meets with from a confessor who is so discreet and has so little experience that there is nothing he is sure of: he fears everything and finds in everything something to doubt, because he sees these unusual experiences. He becomes especially doubtful if he notices some imperfection in a soul that has them, for it seems to such confessors that the ones to whom God grants these favors must be angels—but that is impossible as long as they are in this body. Everything is immediately condemned as from the devil or melancholy. And the world is so full of this melancholy that I am not surprised. There is so much of it now in the world, and the devil causes so many evils through this means that confessors are very right in fearing it and considering it carefully. But the poor soul that walks with the same fear and goes to its confessor as to its judge, and is condemned by him, cannot help but be deeply tormented and disturbed. Only the one who has passed through this will understand what a great torment it is. For this is another one of the terrible trials these souls suffer, especially if they have lived wretched lives, thinking that because of their sins God will allow them to be deceived. Even though they feel secure and cannot believe that the favor, when granted by His Majesty, is from any spirit other than God, the torment returns immediately, since the favor is something that passes quickly, the remembrance of sins is always present, and the soul sees faults in itself, which are never lacking. When the confessor assures it, the soul grows calm, although the disturbance will return. But when the confessor contributes to the torment with more fear, this trial becomes something almost unbearable—especially when some dryness comes between the times of these favors. It then seems to the soul that it has never been mindful of God and never will be; and when it hears His Majesty spoken of, it seems to it as though it were hearing about a person far away.

All this would amount to nothing if it were not for the fact that in addition comes the feeling that it is incapable of explaining things to its confessors, that it has deceived them. And even though it thinks and sees that it tells its confessors about every stirring, even the first ones, this doesn't help. The soul's understanding is so darkened that it becomes incapable of seeing the truth and believes whatever the imagination represents to it (for the imagination is then its master) or whatever foolish things the devil wants to represent. The Lord, it seems, gives the devil license so that the soul might be tried and even be made to think it is rejected by God. Many are the things that war against it with an interior oppression so keen and unbearable that I don't know what to compare this experience to, if not to the oppression of those that suffer in hell, for no consolation is allowed in the midst of this tempest. If they desire to be consoled by their confessor, it seems the devils assist him to torment it more. Thus, when a confessor was dealing with a person after she had suffered this torment (for it seems a dangerous affliction, since there are so many things involved in it), he told her to let him know when she was in this state; but the torment was always so bad that he came to realize there was nothing he could do about it. Well, then, if a person in this state who knows how to read well takes up a book in the vernacular, he will find that he understands no more of it than if he didn't know how to read even one of the letters, for the intellect is incapable of understanding.

In sum, there is no remedy in this tempest but to wait for the mercy of God. For at an unexpected time, with one word alone or a chance happening, he so quickly calms the storm that it seems there had not been even as much as a cloud in that soul, and it remains filled with sunlight and much more consolation. And like one who has escaped from a dangerous battle and been victorious, it comes out praising our Lord; for it was he who fought for the victory. It knows very clearly that it did not fight, for all the weapons with which it could have defended itself are seen to be, it seems, in the hands of its enemies. Thus, it knows clearly its wretchedness and the very little we of ourselves can do if the Lord abandons us.

It seems the soul has no longer any need of reflection to understand this, for the experience of having suffered through it, having seen itself totally incapacitated, made it understand our nothingness and what miserable things we are. For in this state grace is so hidden (even though the soul must not be without grace, since with all this torment it doesn't offend God, nor would it offend him for anything on earth) that not even a very tiny spark is visible. The soul doesn't think that it has any love of God or that it ever had any, for if it has done some good or His Majesty has granted it some favor, all of this seems to have been dreamed up or fancied. As for sins, it sees certainly that it has committed them.

O Jesus, and what a thing it is to see this kind of forsaken soul; and, as I have said, what little help any earthly consolation is for it! Hence, do not think, sisters, if at some time you find yourselves in this state, that the rich and those who are free will have a better remedy for these times of suffering. Absolutely not, for being rich in this case seems to me like the situation of a person condemned to die who has all the world's delights placed before him. These delights would not be sufficient to alleviate his suffering; rather, they would increase the torment. So it is with this torment; it comes from above, and earthly things are of no avail in the matter. Our great God wants us to know our own misery and that he is King; and this is very important for what lies ahead.

Well, then, what will this poor soul do when the torment goes on for many days? If it prays, it feels as though it hasn't prayed— as far as consolation goes, I mean. For consolation is not admitted into the soul's interior, nor is what one recites to oneself, even though vocal, understood. As for mental prayer, this definitely is not the time for that, because the faculties are incapable of the practice; rather, solitude causes greater harm—and also another torment for this soul is that it be with anyone or that others speak to it. And thus, however much it forces itself not to do so, it goes about with a discontented and ill-tempered mien that is exter-nally very noticeable.

Is it true that it will know how to explain its experiences? They are indescribable, for they are spiritual afflictions and sufferings that one doesn't know what to call. The best remedy (I don't mean for getting rid of them, because I don't find any, but so that they may be endured) is to engage in external works of charity and to hope in the mercy of God, who never fails those who hope in him. May he be forever blessed, amen.

Other exterior trials the devils cause must be quite unusual; and so there's no reason to speak of them. Nor are they, for the most part, so painful; for, however much the devils do, they do not, in my opinion, manage to disable the faculties or disturb the soul in this way. In sum, there's reason for thinking that they can do no more than what the Lord allows them to do; and provided one doesn't lose one's mind, everything is small in comparison with what was mentioned.

We shall be speaking in these dwelling places of other interior sufferings and dealing with different kinds of prayer and favors from the Lord. For even though some favors cause still more severe suffering than those mentioned, as will be seen from the condition in which the body is left, they do not deserve to be called trials. Nor is there any reason for us to write of them, since they are such great favors from the Lord. In the midst of receiving them the soul understands that they are great favors and far beyond its merits. This severe suffering comes so that one may enter the seventh dwelling place. It comes along with many other sufferings, only some of which I shall speak of, because it would be impossible to speak of them all, or even to explain what they are; for they are of a different, much higher level than those mentioned in this chapter. And if I haven't been able to explain any more than I did about those of a lower kind, less will I be able to say of the others. May the Lord give his help for everything through the merits of his Son, amen.

Chapter 2

*Deals with some of the ways in which our Lord awakens
the soul. It seems that there is nothing
in these awakenings to fear, even though the
experience is sublime and the favors are
great.*

Seemingly we have left the little dove [or butterfly] far behind;
but we have not, for these are the trials that make it fly still
higher. Well, let us begin, then, to discuss the manner in which
the Spouse deals with it and how, before he belongs to it completely, he makes it desire him vehemently by certain delicate
means the soul itself does not understand. (Nor do I believe I'll
be successful in explaining them, save to those who have experienced them.) These are impulses so delicate and refined, for they
proceed from very deep within the interior part of the soul, that
I don't know any comparison that will fit.

They are far different from all that we can acquire of ourselves here below and even from the spiritual delights that were
mentioned. For often when a person is distracted and forgetful
of God, His Majesty will awaken it. His action is as quick as a
falling comet. And as with a thunderclap, even though no sound
is heard, the soul understands very clearly that it was called by
God. So well does it understand that sometimes, especially in
the beginning, it is made to tremble and even complain without
there being anything that causes it pain. It feels that it is

wounded in the most delightful way, but it doesn't learn how or by whom it was wounded. It knows clearly that the wound is something precious, and it would never want to be cured. It complains to its Spouse with words of love, even outwardly, without being able to do otherwise. It knows that he is present, but he doesn't want to reveal the manner in which he allows himself to be enjoyed. And the pain is great, although delightful and sweet. And even if the soul does not want this wound, the wound cannot be avoided. But the soul, in fact, would never want to be deprived of this pain. The wound satisfies it much more than the delightful and painless absorption of the prayer of quiet.

I am struggling, sisters, to explain for you this action of love, and I don't know how. For it seems a contradiction that the Beloved would give the soul clear understanding that he is with it and yet make it think that he is calling it by a sign so certain that no room is left for doubt and a whisper so penetrating that the soul cannot help but hear it. For it seems that when the Spouse, who is in the seventh dwelling place, communicates in this manner (for the words are not spoken), all the people in the other dwelling places keep still; neither the senses, nor the imagination, nor the faculties stir.

O my powerful God, how sublime are your secrets, and how different spiritual things are from all that is visible and understandable here below. There is nothing that serves to explain this favor, even though the favor is a very small one when compared with the very great ones you work in souls.

This action of love is so powerful that the soul dissolves with desire, and yet it doesn't know what to ask for, since clearly it thinks that its God is with it.

You will ask me: Well, if it knows this, what does it desire or what pains it? What greater good does it want? I don't know. I do know that it seems this pain reaches to the soul's very depths and that when he who wounds it draws out the arrow, it indeed seems in accord with the deep love the soul feels that God is drawing these very depths after him. I was thinking now that it's as though from this fire enkindled in the brazier that is my God a spark leapt forth and so struck the soul that the flaming fire was felt by it. And since the spark was not enough to set the soul on fire, and the fire is so delightful, the soul is left with that pain; but the spark merely by touching the soul produces that effect. It seems to me this is the best comparison I have come up with. This delightful pain—and it is not pain—is not continuous, although sometimes it lasts a long while; at other times it goes away quickly. This depends on the way the Lord wishes to communicate it, for it is not something that can be procured in any human way. But even though it sometimes lasts for a long while, it comes and goes. To sum up, it is never permanent. For this reason it doesn't set the soul on fire; but just as the fire is about to start, the spark goes out and the soul is left with the desire to suffer again that loving pain the spark causes.

Here there is no reason to wonder whether the experience is brought on naturally or caused by melancholy, or whether it is some trick of the devil or some illusion. It is something that leaves clear understanding of how this activity comes from the place where the Lord, who is unchanging, dwells. The activity is not like that found in other feelings of devotion, where the great absorption in delight can make us doubtful. Here all the senses and faculties remain free of any absorption, wondering what this could be, without hindering anything or being able, in my opinion, to increase or take away that delightful pain.

Anyone to whom our Lord may have granted this favor—for if he has, that fact will be recognized on reading this—should thank him very much. Such a person doesn't have to fear deception. Let his great fear be that he might prove ungrateful for so generous a favor, and let him strive to better his entire life and to serve, and he will see the results and how he receives more and more. In fact, I know a person who received this favor for some years and was so pleased with it that, had she served the Lord through severe trials for a great number of years, she would have felt well repaid by it. May he be blessed forever, amen.

You may wonder why greater security is present in this favor than in other things. In my opinion, these are the reasons. First, the devil never gives delightful pain like this. He can give the savor and delight that seem to be spiritual, but he doesn't have the power to join pain—and so much of it—to the spiritual quiet and delight of the soul. For all of his powers are on the outside, and the pains he causes are never, in my opinion, delightful or peaceful, but disturbing and contentious. Second, this delightful tempest comes from a region other than those regions of which he can be lord. Third, the favor brings wonderful benefits to the soul, the more customary of which are the determination to suffer for God, the desire to have many trials, and the determination to withdraw from earthly satisfactions and conversations and other similar things.

That this favor is no fancy is very clear. Although at other times the soul may strive to experience this favor, it will not be able to counterfeit one. And the impulse is something so manifest that it can in no way be fancied. I mean, one cannot think it is imagined, when it is not, or have doubts about it. If some doubt should remain, one must realize that the things experienced are not true impulses—I mean, if there should be doubt about whether the favor was experienced or not. The favor is felt as clearly as a loud voice is heard. There's no basis for thinking it is caused by melancholy, because melancholy does not produce or fabricate its fancies save in the imagination. This favor proceeds from the interior part of the soul.

Now, it could be that I'm mistaken, but until I hear other reasons from someone who understands the experience, I will always have this opinion. I know a person who was quite fearful about being deceived, but who never had any fear of this prayer.

The Lord also has other ways of awakening the soul: unexpectedly when it is praying vocally and without thinking of anything interior, it seems a delightful enkindling will come upon it, as though a fragrance were suddenly to become so powerful as to spread through all the senses. (I don't say that it is a fragrance but am merely making this comparison.) Or the experience is something like this, and it is communicated only for the sake of making one feel the Spouse's presence there. It moves the soul to a delightful desire of enjoying him, and thereby the soul is prepared to make intense acts of love and praise of our Lord. This favor rises out of that place I mentioned; but there is nothing in it that causes pain, nor are the desires themselves to enjoy God painful. Such is the way the soul usually experiences it. Neither does it seem to me, for some of the reasons mentioned, there is anything to fear; but one should try to receive this favor with gratitude.

Chapter 3

Deals with the same subject and tells of the manner in which God, when pleased, speaks to the soul. Gives counsel about how one should behave in such a matter and not follow one's own opinion. Sets down some signs for discerning when there is deception and when not. This chapter is very beneficial.

God has another way of awakening the soul. Although it some-how seems to be a greater favor than those mentioned, it can be more dangerous, and therefore I shall spend some time consid-ering it. There are many kinds of locutions given to the soul. Some seem to come from outside oneself; others, from deep within the interior part of the soul; others, from the superior part; and some are so exterior that they come through the sense of hearing, for it seems there is a spoken word. Sometimes, and

often, the locution can be an illusion, especially in persons with
a weak imagination or in those who are melancholic, I mean,
who suffer noticeably from melancholy.

In my opinion, no attention should be paid to these latter two
kinds of persons even if they say they see and hear and understand. But neither should one disturb these persons by telling
them their locutions come from the devil; one must listen to
them as to sick persons. The prioress or confessor to whom they
relate their locutions should tell them to pay no attention to such
experiences, that these locutions are not essential to the service of
God, and that the devil has deceived many by such means, even
though this particular person, perhaps, may not be suffering such
deception. This counsel should be given so as not to aggravate the
melancholy, for if they tell her the locution is due to melancholy,
there will be no end to the matter; she will swear that she sees
and hears, for it seems to her that she does.

It is true that it's necessary to be firm in taking prayer away
from her and to insist strongly that she pay no attention to locutions; for the devil is wont to profit from these souls that are sick
in this way, even though what he does may not be to their harm,
but to the harm of others. But for both the sick and the healthy
there is always reason to fear these things until the spirit of such
persons is well understood. And I say that in the beginning it is
always better to free these persons from such experiences, for if
the locutions are from God, doing so is a greater help toward
progress, and a person even grows when tested. This is true;
nonetheless, one should not proceed in a way that is distressing

or disturbing to a soul, because truly the soul can't help it if these locutions come.

Now then, to return to what I was saying about locutions, all the kinds I mentioned can be from God or from the devil or from one's own imagination. If I can manage to do so, I shall give, with the help of the Lord, the signs as to when they come from these different sources and when they are dangerous; for there are many souls among prayerful people who hear them. My desire, sisters, is that you realize you are doing the right thing if you refuse to give credence to them, even when they are destined just for you (such as some consolation, or advice about your faults), no matter who tells you about them, or if they are an illusion, for it doesn't matter where they come from. One thing I advise you: do not think, even if the locutions are from God, that you are better because of them, for he spoke frequently with the Pharisees. All the good comes from how one benefits by these words; and pay no more attention to those that are not in close conformity with Scripture than you would to those heard from the devil himself. Even if they come from your weak imagination, it's necessary to treat them as if they were temptations in matters of faith, and thus resist them always. They will then go away, because they will have little effect on you.

Returning, then, to the first of the different kinds of locutions; whether or not the words come from the interior part of the soul, from the superior part, or from the exterior part doesn't matter in discerning whether or not they are from God. The surest signs they are from God that can be had, in my opinion, are these: the first and truest is the power and authority they bear, for locutions from God effect what they say. Let me explain myself better. A soul finds itself in the midst of all the tribulation and disturbance that was mentioned, in darkness of the intellect and in dryness; with one word alone of these that the Lord says ("Don't be distressed"), it is left calm and free from all distress, with great light, and without all that suffering in which it seemed to it that all the learned men and all who might come together to give it reasons for not being distressed would be unable to remove its affliction, no matter how hard they tried. Or it is afflicted because its confessor and others have told it that its spirit is from the devil, and it is all full of fear; with one word alone ("It is I, fear not"), the fear is taken away completely, and the soul is most comforted, thinking that nothing would be sufficient to make it believe anything else. Or it is greatly distressed over how certain serious business matters will turn out; it hears that it should be calm, that everything will turn out all right. It is left certain and free of anxiety. And this is the way in many other instances.

The second sign is the great quiet left in the soul, the devout and peaceful recollection, the readiness to engage in the praises of God. O Lord, if a word sent to be spoken through one of your attendants (for the Lord himself does not speak the words—at least not in this dwelling place—but an angel) has such power, what will be the power you leave in the soul that is attached to you, and you to it, through love?

The third sign is that these words remain in the memory for a very long time, and some are never forgotten, as are those we listen to here on earth—I mean, those we hear from men. For even if the words are spoken by men who are very important and learned, or concern the future, we do not have them engraved on our memory, or believe them, as we do these. The certitude is so strong that, even in things that in one's own opinion sometimes seem impossible and there is doubt as to whether they will or will not happen, and the intellect wavers, there is an assurance in the soul itself that cannot be overcome. Even though it seems that everything is going contrary to what the soul understood, and years go by, the thought remains that God will find other means than those men know of and that in the end the words will be accomplished; and so they are. Although, as I say, the soul still suffers when it sees the many delays, for since time has passed since it heard the words, and the effects and the certitude that were present about their being from God have passed, these doubts take place. The soul wonders whether the locutions might have come from the devil or from the imagination. Yet none of these doubts remain in the soul, but it would at present die a thousand deaths for that truth. But, as I say, what won't the devil do with all these imaginings so as to afflict and intimidate the soul, especially if the words regard a business matter that, when carried out, will bring many blessings to souls, and works that will bring great honor and service to God, and if there is great difficulty involved? At least he weakens faith, for it does great harm not to believe that God has the power to do things that our intellects do not understand.

Despite all these struggles and even the persons who tell one that the locutions are foolishness (I mean, the confessors with

whom one speaks about these things), and despite the many
unfortunate occurrences that make it seem the words will not be
fulfilled, there remains a spark of assurance so alive—I don't
know from where—that the words will be fulfilled, though all
other hopes are dead, that even should the soul desire otherwise,
that spark will stay alive. And in the end, as I have said, the words
of the Lord are fulfilled, and the soul is so consoled and happy
that it wouldn't want to do anything but always praise His
Majesty and praise him more for the fact that what he had told it
was fulfilled than for the work itself, no matter how important
the work is to the soul.

I don't know why it is so important to the soul that these
words turn out to be true, for if that soul were itself caught in
some lies, I don't think it would regret the fact as much. And yet
there is nothing else it can do, for it merely says what it hears.
Countless times, in this regard, a certain person thought of how
the prophet Jonah feared that Nineveh would not be destroyed
[Jon. 1; 4]. In sum, since the spirit is from God, it is right that
the soul be faithful in its desire that the words be considered
true, for God is the supreme truth. And so its happiness is great
when, through a thousand roundabout ways and in most difficult circumstances, it sees them fulfilled. Even though great trials should come to the person herself from them, she would
rather suffer such trials than the trial of seeing that what the
Lord told her fails in fact to happen. Perhaps not all persons will
have this weakness—if it is a weakness, for I cannot condemn it
as bad.

If the locutions come from the imagination, there are none of these signs; neither certitude, nor peace, nor interior delight. But it could happen—and I even know some persons to whom it has happened—that while these imaginings come, a person may be very absorbed in the prayer of quiet and spiritual sleep. Some have such a weak constitution and imagination, or I don't know the cause, that indeed in this deep recollection they are so outside themselves (for they don't feel anything exteriorly and all the senses are put to sleep) that they think as when they are asleep and dreaming (and perhaps it is true that they are asleep) that these locutions are spoken to them and even that they see things. And they think these things are from God, but in the end the effects are like those of sleep. It can also happen that while with affection they are begging our Lord for something, they think the locution is telling them what they want to hear; this sometimes happens. But anyone who has had much experience of God's locutions will not be deceived by these that come, in my opinion, from the imagination.

With those locutions coming from the devil there is more to fear. But if the signs mentioned are present, there can be a great deal of certainty that the locutions are from God. But the certainty shouldn't be so strong that, if the locution concerns something serious about oneself and has to be carried out in deed or business affairs involving third parties, anything should ever be done or pass through one's mind without the opinion of a learned and prudent confessor and servant of God. This is so even if the soul increasingly understands and thinks the locution is clearly from God. His Majesty wants the soul to consult in this way; and that it does so does not mean it is failing to carry out the Lord's commands, for he has told us, where the words are undoubtedly his, to hold the confessor in his place [Luke 10:16]. And these words of his help to give courage if the task is a difficult one, and our Lord, when he so desires, will make the confessor believe that the locution comes from his spirit. If he doesn't, the confessor and the soul are no longer under obligation. To do otherwise and follow nothing but your own opinion in this I hold to be very dangerous. And so, sisters, I warn you, on the part of our Lord, that this never happen to you.

There is another way in which the Lord speaks to the soul—for I hold that it is very definitely from him—with a certain intellectual vision, the nature of which I will explain farther on. The locution takes place in such intimate depths and a person with the ears of the soul seems to hear those words from the Lord himself so clearly and so in secret that this very way in which they are heard, together with the acts that the vision itself produces, assures that person and gives him certitude that the devil can have no part to play in the locution. Wonderful effects are left so that the soul may believe; at least there is assurance that the locution doesn't come from the imagination. Furthermore, if the soul is attentive, it can always have assurance for the following reasons. First, there is a difference because of the clarity of the locution. It is so clear that the soul remembers every syllable and whether it is said in one style or another, even if it is a whole sentence. But in a locution fancied by the imagination the words will not be so clear or distinct, but like something half dreamed.

Second, in these locutions one often is not thinking about what is heard (I mean, that it comes unexpectedly and even sometimes while one is in conversation), although many times it is a response to what passes quickly through the mind or to what did so previously. But it often refers to things about the future that never entered the mind, and so the imagination couldn't have fabricated it in such a way that the soul could be deceived in fancying what was not desired or wanted or thought of.

Third, the one locution comes as in the case of a person who hears, and that of imagination comes as in the case of a person who gradually composes what he himself wants to be told.

Fourth, the words are very different, and with one of them much is comprehended. Our intellect could not compose them so quickly.

Fifth, together with the words, in a way I wouldn't know how to explain, there is often given much more to understand than is ever dreamed of without words.

I shall speak more about this mode of understanding elsewhere, for it is something very delicate and to the praise of our Lord. For in regard to these different kinds of locutions, there have been persons who were very doubtful and unable to understand themselves. A certain person, especially, experienced this doubt, and so there will be others. And thus I know that she observed the differences with close attention, because the Lord has often granted her this favor, and the greatest doubt she had in the beginning was whether she had imagined the locution. That the words come from the devil can be more quickly understood, even though his wiles are so many, for he knows well how to counterfeit the Spirit of light. In my opinion the devil will say the words very clearly, so that there will be certitude about their meaning, as is so with those coming from the Spirit of truth. But he will not be able to counterfeit the effects that were mentioned or leave this peace or light in the soul; on the contrary, he leaves restlessness and disturbance. But he can do little or no harm if the soul is humble and does what I have mentioned, that is, doesn't make a move to do a thing of what it hears.

If the locutions contain words of favor and consolation from the Lord, let the soul look attentively to see if it thinks that, because of them, it is better than others. The more it hears words of favor, the more humble it should be left; if it isn't, let it believe that the spirit is not from God. One thing very certain is that when the spirit is from God, the soul esteems itself less, the greater the favor he granted, and it has more awareness of its sins and is more forgetful of its own gain, and its will and memory are employed more in seeking only the honor of God; nor does it think about its own profit, and it walks with greater fear, lest its will deviate in anything, and with greater certitude that it never deserved any of those favors but deserved hell. Since all the favors and things it experienced in prayer produce these effects, the soul does not walk fearfully, but with confidence in the mercy of the Lord, who is faithful [1 Cor. 10:13] and will not let the devil deceive it; although walking with fear is always good.

It could be that those whom the Lord does not lead along this path think that such souls could refuse to listen to these words spoken to them—and, if the words are interior, distract themselves in such a way that they not be admitted—and as a result go about free of these dangers.

To this I reply that it is impossible. I'm not speaking of imaginary locutions, for by not being so desirous of a thing or wanting to pay attention to their imaginings souls have a remedy. In locutions from the Lord, they have none. For the very spirit that speaks puts a stop to all other thoughts and makes the soul attend to what is said. It does this in such a way that I think, and I believe truly, that somehow it would be more possible for a person with very good hearing not to hear someone else speaking in a loud voice. In this latter instance the person would be able to turn his attention away and center his mind and intellect on something else. But in the locution we are speaking about this cannot be done; there are no ears to stop, nor is there the power to think of anything but what is said to the soul. For he who was able to stop the sun (through Joshua's prayer, I believe [Josh. 10:12–13]), can make the faculties and the whole interior stop in such a way that the soul sees clearly that another, greater Lord than itself governs that castle. And this brings it deep devotion and humility. So there's no remedy for this kind of locution. May the divine Majesty provide a remedy that will enable us to place our eyes only on pleasing him and to be forgetful of ourselves, as I said, amen.

Please God that I may have succeeded in explaining what I set out to; may it be helpful for whoever has had such experience.

Chapter 4

Treats when God suspends the soul in prayer
with rapture or ecstasy or transport, which are
all the same in my opinion, and how great
courage is necessary to receive sublime favors
from His Majesty.

With these trials and the other things that were mentioned, what kind of calm can the poor little butterfly have? All these sufferings are meant to increase one's desire to enjoy the Spouse. And His Majesty, as one who knows our weakness, is enabling the soul through these afflictions and many others to have the courage to be joined with so great a Lord and to take him as its Spouse.

You will laugh at my saying this and will think it's foolishness; it will seem to any one of you that such courage is unnecessary and that there's no woman so miserable who wouldn't have the courage to be married to the king. I believe this is true with respect to kings here on earth; but with respect to the King of heaven, I tell you there is need for more courage than you think. Our nature is very timid and lowly when it comes to something so great, and I am certain that if God were not to give the courage, no matter how much you might see that the favor is good for us, it would be impossible for you to receive that favor. And thus you will see what His Majesty does to conclude this betrothal, which I understand must be established when he gives the soul raptures that draw it out of its senses. For if it were to see

itself so near this great majesty while in its senses, it would perhaps die. Let it be understood that I mean true raptures and not
the weaknesses women experience here below, for everything
seems to us to be a rapture or an ecstasy. And, as I believe I have
said, some have constitutions so weak that the prayer of quiet is
enough to make them die.

I want to put down here some kinds of rapture that I've come
to understand, because I've discussed them with so many spiritual persons. But I don't know whether I shall succeed as I did
when I wrote elsewhere about them and other things that occur
in this dwelling place. On account of certain reasons it seems
worthwhile to speak of these kinds of rapture again—if for no
other reason, so that everything related to these dwelling places
will be put down here together.

One kind of rapture is that in which the soul, even though not
in prayer, is touched by some word it remembers or hears about
God. It seems that His Majesty from the interior of the soul makes
the spark we mentioned increase, for he is moved with compas-
sion in seeing the soul suffer so long a time from its desire. All
burned up, the soul is renewed like the phoenix, and one can
devoutly believe that its faults are pardoned. Now that it is so
pure, the Lord joins it with himself, without anyone understanding what is happening except these two; nor does the soul itself
understand in a way that can afterward be explained. Yet it does
have interior understanding, for this experience is not like that of
fainting or convulsion; in these latter nothing is understood
inwardly or outwardly.

What I know in this case is that the soul was never so awake to the things of God, nor did it have such deep enlightenment and knowledge of His Majesty. This will seem impossible, for if the faculties are so absorbed that we can say they are dead, and likewise the senses, how can a soul know that it understands this secret? I don't know, nor perhaps does any creature, but only the Creator. And this goes for many other things that take place in this state—I mean, in these two dwelling places, for there is no closed door between the one and the other. Because there are things in the last that are not revealed to those who have not yet reached it, I thought I should divide them.

When the soul is in this suspension, the Lord likes to show it some secrets, things about heaven, and imaginative visions. It is able to tell of them afterward, for these remain so impressed on the memory that they are never forgotten. But when the visions are intellectual, the soul doesn't know how to speak of them. For there must be some visions during these moments that are so sublime that it's not fitting for those who live on this earth to have the further understanding necessary to explain them. However, since the soul is in possession of its senses, it can say many things about these intellectual visions.

It could be that some of you do not know what a vision is, especially an intellectual one. I shall explain at the proper time, for one who has the authority ordered me to do so. And although the explanation may not seem pertinent, it will perhaps benefit some souls.

Well, now, you will ask me: If afterward there is to be no remembrance of these sublime favors granted by the Lord to the soul in this state, what benefit do they have? O daughters, they are so great one cannot exaggerate! For even though they are unexplainable, they are well inscribed in the very interior part of the soul and are never forgotten.

But, you will insist, if there is no image and the faculties do not understand, how can the visions be remembered? I don't understand this either; but I do understand that some truths about the grandeur of God remain so fixed in this soul that, even if faith were not to tell it who God is and of its obligation to believe that he is God, from that very moment it would adore him as God, as did Jacob when he saw the ladder. By means of the ladder Jacob must have understood other secrets that he didn't know how to explain, for by seeing just a ladder on which angels descended and ascended [Gen. 28:12], he would not have understood such great mysteries if there had not been deeper interior enlightenment. I don't know if I'm guessing right in what I say, for although I have heard this story about Jacob, I don't know if I'm remembering it correctly.

Nor did Moses know how to describe all that he saw in the bush, but only what God wished him to describe [Exod. 3:1–16]. But if God had not shown secrets to his soul along with a certitude that made him recognize and believe that they were from God, Moses could not have entered into so many severe trials. But he must have understood such deep things among the thorns of that bush, that the vision gave him the courage to do what he did for the people of Israel. So, sisters, we don't have to look for reasons to understand the hidden things of God. Since we believe he is powerful, clearly we must believe that a worm with as limited a power as ours will not understand his grandeurs. Let us praise him, for he is pleased that we come to know some of them.

I have been wanting to find some comparison by which to explain what I'm speaking about, and I don't think there is any that fits. But let's use this one. You enter into the room of a king or great lord, or I believe they call it the treasure chamber, where there are countless kinds of glass and earthen vessels and other things so arranged that almost all of these objects are seen upon entering. Once I was brought to a room like this in the house of the Duchess of Alba, where, while I was on a journey, obedience ordered me to stay because of this lady's insistence with my superiors. I was amazed on entering and wondered what gain could be gotten from that conglomeration of things, and I saw that one could praise the Lord at seeing so many different kinds of objects, and now I laugh to myself on realizing how the experience has helped me here in my explanation. Although I was in that room for a while, there was so much there to see that I soon forgot it all; none of those pieces has remained in my memory any more than if I had never seen them, nor would I know how to explain the workmanship of any of them. I can only say in general that I remember seeing everything. Likewise with this favor, the soul, while it is made one with God, is placed in this empyreal room that we must have interiorly. For, clearly, the soul has some of these dwelling places, since God abides within it. And although the Lord must not want the soul to see these secrets every time it is in this ecstasy, for it can be so absorbed in enjoying him that a sublime good like that is sufficient for it, sometimes he is pleased that the absorption decrease and the soul see at once what is in that room. After it returns to itself, the soul is left with that representation of the grandeurs it saw; but it cannot describe any of them, nor do its natural powers grasp any more than what God wished that it see supernaturally.

You, therefore, might object that I admit that the soul sees and that the vision is an imaginative one. But I'm not saying that, for I'm not dealing with an imaginative vision, but with an intellectual one. Since I have no learning, I don't know how in my dullness to explain anything. If what I have said up to now about this prayer is worthwhile, I know clearly that I'm not the one who has said it.

I hold that if at times in its raptures the soul doesn't understand these secrets, its raptures are not given by God, but are caused by some natural weakness. It can happen to persons with a weak constitution, as is so with women, that any spiritual force will overcome the natural powers, and the soul will be absorbed, as I believe I mentioned in reference to the prayer of quiet. These experiences have nothing to do with rapture. In a rapture, believe me, God carries off for himself the entire soul, and, as to someone who is his own and his spouse, he begins showing it some little part of the kingdom that it has gained by being espoused to him. However small that part of his kingdom may be, everything that there is in this great God is magnificent. And he doesn't want any hindrance from anyone, neither from the faculties nor from the senses, but he immediately commands the doors of all these dwelling places to be closed; and only that door to his room remains open so that we can enter. Blessed be so much mercy; they will be rightly cursed who have not wanted to benefit by it and who have lost this Lord.

O my sisters, what nothingness it is, that which we leave! Nor is what we do anything, nor all that we could do for a God who thus wishes to communicate himself to a worm! And if we hope to enjoy this blessing even in this present life, what are we doing? What is causing us to delay? What is enough to make us, even momentarily, stop looking for this Lord as did the bride in the streets and in the squares [Song of Sol. 3:2]? Oh, what a mockery everything in the world is, if it doesn't lead us and help us toward this blessing, even if its delights and riches and joys, as much of them as imaginable, were to last forever! It is all loathsome dung compared to these treasures that will be enjoyed without end. Nor are these anything in comparison with having as our own the Lord of all the treasures of heaven and earth.

O human blindness! How long, how long before this dust will be removed from our eyes! Even though among ourselves the dust doesn't seem to be capable of blinding us completely, I see some specks, some tiny pebbles that, if we allow them to increase, will be enough to do us great harm. On the contrary, for the love of God, sisters, let us benefit by these faults so as to know our misery, and they will give us clearer vision as did the mud to the blind man cured by our Spouse [John 9:6–7]. Thus, seeing ourselves so imperfect, let us increase our supplications that His Majesty may draw good out of our miseries so that we might be pleasing to him.

I have digressed a great deal without realizing it. Pardon me, sisters, and believe me that, having reached these grandeurs of God (I mean, reached the place where I must speak of them), I cannot help but feel very sorry to see what we lose through our own fault. Even though it is true that these are blessings the Lord gives to whomever he wills, His Majesty would give them all to us if we loved him as he loves us. He doesn't desire anything else than to have those to whom to give. His riches do not lessen because he gives them away.

Well, now, to get back to what I was saying, the Spouse commands that the doors of the dwelling places be closed and even those of the castle and the outer wall. For in desiring to carry off this soul, he takes away the breath so that, even though the other senses sometimes last a little longer, a person cannot speak at all; although at other times everything is taken away at once, and the hands and the body grow cold so that the person doesn't seem to have any life; nor sometimes is it known whether he is breathing. This situation lasts but a short while, I mean, in its intensity; for when this extreme suspension lets up a little, it seems that the body returns to itself somewhat and is nourished so as to die again and give more life to the soul. Nevertheless, so extreme an ecstasy doesn't last long.

But it will happen that even though the extreme ecstasy ends, the will remains so absorbed and the intellect so withdrawn, for a day and even days, that the latter seems incapable of understanding anything that doesn't lead to awakening the will to love; and the will is wide awake to this love and asleep to becoming attached to any creature.

Oh, when the soul returns completely to itself, what bewilderment and how intense its desires to be occupied in God in every kind of way he might want! If the effects that were mentioned were produced by the former kinds of prayer, what will be the effects of a favor as sublime as this? The soul would desire to have a thousand lives so as to employ them all for God and that everything here on earth would be a tongue to help it praise him. The desires to do penance are most strong, but not much help comes from performing it, because the strength of love makes the soul feel that all that is done amounts to little and see clearly that the martyrs did not accomplish much in suffering the torments they did, because with this help from our Lord such suffering is easy. Hence these souls complain to His Majesty when no opportunity for suffering presents itself.

When this favor is granted them in secret their esteem for it is great; when it is given in the presence of other persons their embarrassment and shame are so strong that the pain and worry over what those who saw it will think somehow take the soul away from what was being enjoyed. For these persons know the malice of the world, and they understand that the world will not perhaps regard the experience for what it is, but that what the Lord should be praised for will perhaps be the occasion for rash judgments. In some ways it seems to me that this pain and embarrassment amount to a lack of humility, for if this person desires to be reviled, what difference does it make what others think? But the soul cannot control such feelings. One who was in this affliction heard from the Lord: "Don't be afflicted. Either they will praise me or criticize you, and in either case you gain." I learned afterward that this person was very much consoled and encouraged by these words, and I put them down here in case one of you might find herself in this affliction. It seems that our Lord wishes all to understand that that soul is now his, that no one should touch it. Well and good if its body, or honor, or possessions are touched, for this soul draws honor for His Majesty out of everything. But that one touch the soul—absolutely not; for if the soul does not withdraw from its Spouse through a very culpable boldness, he will protect it from the whole world and even from all hell.

I don't know if anything has been explained about the nature of rapture, for to explain it is completely impossible, as I have said. But I don't believe anything has been lost by trying. For there are effects that are very different in feigned raptures. I do not say "feigned" because the one who has the experience wants to deceive, but because that person is deceived. And since the signs and effects of the feigned raptures are not in conformity with such a great blessing, the true rapture is looked on unfavorably; and afterward the one to whom the Lord grants it justifiably is not believed. May he be blessed and praised forever, amen, amen.

Chapter 5

Continues on the same subject and deals
with a kind of rapture in which God raises
up the soul through a flight of the spirit,
an experience different from that just
explained. Tells why courage is necessary.
Explains something about this delightful
favor the Lord grants. The chapter is a very
beneficial one.

There is another kind of rapture—I call it flight of the spirit—that, though substantially the same as other raptures, is interiorly experienced very differently. For sometimes suddenly a movement of the soul is felt that is so swift it seems the spirit is carried off, and at a fearful speed, especially in the beginning. This is why I have told you that strong courage is necessary for the one to whom God grants these favors, and even faith and confidence and a full surrender to our Lord, so that he may do what he wants with the soul. Do you think it is a small disturbance for a person to be very much in his senses and see his soul carried off (and in the case of some, we have read, even the body with the soul) without knowing where that soul is going, what or who does this, or how? At the beginning of this swift movement there is not so much certitude that the rapture is from God.

Well, now, is there some means by which one can resist it? None at all; rather, to resist makes matters worse, for I know this was so with a certain person. It seems God wishes that the soul that has so often, so earnestly, and with such complete willingness offered everything to him should understand that, in itself, it no longer has any part to play; and it is carried off with a noticeably more impetuous movement. It is determined now to do no more than what the straw does when drawn by the amber—if you have noticed—and abandon itself into the hands of the One who is all-powerful, for it sees that the safest thing to do is to make a virtue of necessity. And that I mentioned a straw is certainly appropriate, for as easily as a huge giant snatches up a straw, this great and powerful Giant of ours carries away the spirit.

It seems that the trough of water we mentioned (I believe it was in the fourth dwelling place, for I don't recall exactly) filled so easily and gently, I mean, without any movement. Here this great God, who holds back the springs of water and doesn't allow the sea to go beyond its boundaries [Prov. 8:29], lets loose the springs from which the water in this trough flows. With a powerful impulse, a huge wave rises up so forcefully that it lifts high this little bark that is our soul. A bark cannot prevent the furious waves from leaving it where they will; nor does the pilot have the power, nor do those who take part in controlling the little ship. So much less can the interior part of the soul stay where it will or make its senses or faculties do other than what they are commanded; here the soul doesn't care what happens outwardly.

It is certain, sisters, that just from writing about it I am amazed at how the immense power of this great King and Emperor is shown here. What will be the amazement of the one who experiences it! I hold that if His Majesty were to reveal this power to those who go astray in the world as he does to these souls, the former would not dare offend him; this out of fear, if not out of love. Oh, how obliged, then, will those persons be who have been informed through so sublime a path to strive with all their might not to displease this Lord! For love of him, sisters, I beg you, those of you to whom His Majesty has granted these favors, or others like them, that you don't grow careless, doing nothing but receiving. Reflect that the one who owes a lot must pay a lot [Luke 12:48].

In this respect, too, great courage is necessary, for this favor is something frightening. If our Lord were not to give such courage, the soul would always go about deeply distressed. For it reflects on what His Majesty does for it and turns back to look at itself, at how little it serves in comparison with its obligation, and at how the tiny bit it does is full of faults, failures, and weaknesses. So as not to recall how imperfectly it performs some work—if it does—it prefers striving to forget its works, keeping in mind its sins, and placing itself before the mercy of God. Since it doesn't have anything with which to pay, it begs for the pity and mercy God has always had toward sinners.

Perhaps he will respond as he did to a person who, before a crucifix, was reflecting with deep affliction that she had never had anything to give to God or anything to give up for him. The Crucified himself in consoling her told her he had given her all the sufferings and trials he had undergone in his Passion, so that she could have them as her own to offer his Father. The comfort and enrichment was such that, according to what I have heard from her, she cannot forget the experience. Rather, every time she sees how miserable she is, she gets encouragement and consolation from remembering those words.

I could mention here some other experiences like this, for since I have dealt with so many holy and prayerful persons, I know about many such experiences; but I want to limit myself lest you think I am speaking of myself. What I said seems to me very beneficial to help you understand how pleased our Lord is that we know ourselves and strive to reflect again and again on our poverty and misery and on how we possess nothing that we have not received. So, my sisters, courage is necessary for this knowledge and for the many other graces given to the soul the Lord has brought to this stage. And when there is humility, courage, in my opinion, is even more necessary for this knowledge of one's own misery. May the Lord give us this humility because of who he is.

Well, now, to return to this quick rapture of the spirit. It is such that the spirit truly seems to go forth from the body. On the other hand, it is clear that this person is not dead; at least, he cannot say whether for some moments he was in the body or not. It seems to him that he was entirely in another region different from this in which we live, where there is shown another light so different from earth's light that if he were to spend his whole life trying to imagine that light, along with the other things, he would be unable to do so. It happens that within an instant so many things together are taught him that, if he were to work for many years with his imagination and mind in order to systematize them, he wouldn't be able to do so, not with even one-thousandth part of one of them. This is not an intellectual but an imaginative vision, for the eyes of the soul see much better than do bodily eyes here on earth, and without words understanding of some things is given; I mean that if a person sees some saints, he knows them as well as if he had often spoken with them.

At other times, along with the things seen through the eyes of the soul by an intellectual vision, other things are represented, especially a multitude of angels with their Lord. And without seeing anything with the eyes of the body or the soul, through an admirable knowledge I will not be able to explain, there is represented what I'm saying and many other things not meant to be spoken of. Anyone who experiences them, and has more ability than I, will perhaps know how to explain them, although doing so seems to me very difficult indeed. Whether all this takes place in the body or not, I wouldn't know; at least I wouldn't swear that the soul is in the body or that the body is without the soul [2 Cor. 12:2–4].

I have often thought that just as the sun while in the sky has such strong rays that, even though it doesn't move from there, the rays promptly reach the earth, so the soul and the spirit, which are one, could be like the sun and its rays. Thus, while the soul remains in its place, the superior part rises above it. In a word, I don't know what I'm saying. What is true is that with the speed of a ball shot from an arquebus, when fire is applied, an interior flight is experienced—I don't know what else to call it—which, though noiseless, is so clearly a movement that it cannot be the work of the imagination. And while the spirit is far outside itself, from all it can understand, great things are shown to it. When it again senses that it is within itself, the benefits it feels are remarkable, and it has so little esteem for all earthly things, in comparison to the things it has seen, that the former seem like dung. From then on its life on earth is very painful, and it doesn't see anything good in those things that used to seem good to it. The experience causes it to care little about them. It seems that the Lord, like those Israelites who brought back signs from the promised land [Num. 13:17–29], has desired to show it something about its future land, so that it may suffer the trials of this laborious path, knowing where it must go to get its final rest. Even though something that passes so quickly will not seem to you very beneficial, the blessings left in the soul are so great that only the person who has this experience will be able to understand its value.

Wherefore, the experience, obviously, is not from the devil; it would be impossible for the imagination or the devil to represent things that leave so much virtue, peace, calm, and improvement in the soul. Three things, especially, are left in it to a very sublime degree: knowledge of the grandeur of God, because the more we see of this grandeur, the greater is our understanding; self-knowledge and humility on seeing that something so low in comparison with the Creator of so many grandeurs dared to offend him (and neither does the soul dare look up at him); the third, little esteem of earthly things save for those that can be used for the service of so great a God.

These are the jewels the Spouse begins to give the betrothed, and their value is such that the soul will not want to lose them.

For these meetings remain so engraved in the memory that I believe it's impossible to forget them until one enjoys them forever, unless they are forgotten through one's own most serious fault. But the Spouse who gives them has the power to give the grace not to lose them.

Well, to get back to the courage that is necessary, does it seem to you that this is so trivial a thing? For it truly seems that because the soul loses its senses and doesn't understand why, it is separated from the body. It's necessary that he who gives everything else give the courage also. You will say that this fear is well paid. So do I. May it please His Majesty to give us the courage so that we may merit to serve him, amen.

Chapter 11

Treats some desires God gives the soul that are
so powerful and vehement they place it in danger
of death. Treats also the benefits caused by this
favor the Lord grants.

Do you think that all these favors the Spouse has bestowed on the soul will be sufficient to satisfy the little dove or butterfly—don't think I have forgotten it—so that it may come to rest in the place where it will die? No, certainly not; rather, this little butterfly is much worse. Even though it may have been receiving these favors for many years, it always moans and goes about sorrowful because they leave it with greater pain. The reason is that, since it is getting to know ever more the grandeurs of its God and sees itself so distant and far from enjoying him, the desire for the Lord increases much more; also, love increases in the measure the soul discovers how much this great God and Lord deserves to be loved. And this desire continues, gradually growing in these years so that it reaches a point of suffering as great as that I shall now speak of. I have said "years" so as to be in line with the experience of that person I've mentioned here, for I well understand that one must not put limits on God; in a moment he can bring a soul to the lofty experience mentioned here. His Majesty has the power to do whatever he wants and is eager to do many things for us.

Well, here is what happens sometimes to a soul that experiences these anxious longings, tears, sighs, and great impulses that were mentioned (for all of these seem to proceed from our love with deep feelings, but they are all nothing in comparison with this other experience that I'm going to explain, for they resemble a smoking fire that, though painful, can be endured). While this soul is going about in this manner, burning up within itself, a blow is felt from elsewhere (the soul doesn't understand from where or how). The blow comes often through a sudden thought or word about death's delay. Or the soul will feel pierced by a fiery arrow. I don't say that there is an arrow, but whatever the experience, the soul realizes clearly that the feeling couldn't come about naturally. Neither is the experience that of a blow, although I said "blow"; but it causes a sharp wound. And, in my opinion, it isn't felt where earthly sufferings are felt, but in the very deep and intimate part of the soul, where this sudden flash of lightning reduces to dust everything it finds in this earthly nature of ours; for while this experience lasts, nothing can be remembered about our being. In an instant the experience so binds the faculties that they have no freedom for anything except those things that will make this pain increase.

I wouldn't want what I say to appear to be an exaggeration. Indeed, I see that my words fall short because the experience is unexplainable. It is an enrapturing of the faculties and senses away from everything that is not a help, as I said, to feeling this affliction. For the intellect is very alive to understanding the reason why the soul feels far from God; and His Majesty helps at that time with a vivid knowledge of himself in such a way that the pain increases to a point that makes the one who experiences it begin to cry aloud. Though she is a person who has suffered and is used to suffering severe pains, she cannot then do otherwise. This feeling is not in the body, as was said, but in the interior part of the soul. As a result, this person understood how much more severe the feelings of the soul are than those of the body, and she reflected that such must be the nature of the sufferings of souls in purgatory, for the fact that these souls have no body doesn't keep them from suffering much more than they do through all the bodily sufferings they endure here on earth.

I saw a person in this condition; truly she thought she was dying, and this was not so surprising, because certainly there is great danger of death. And thus, even though the experience lasts a short while, it leaves the body very disjointed, and during that time the heartbeat is as slow as it would be if a person were about to render his soul to God. This is no exaggeration, for the natural heat fails, and the fire so burns the soul that with a little more intensity God would have fulfilled the soul's desires. This is true not because a person feels little or much pain in the body, although it is disjointed, as I said, in such a way that for three or four days afterward one feels great sufferings and doesn't even have the strength to write. And it even seems to me always that the body is left weaker. The reason one doesn't feel the pain must be that the interior feeling of the soul is so much greater that one doesn't pay any attention to the body. When one experiences a very sharp bodily pain, other bodily pains are hardly felt, even though there may be many. I have indeed experienced this. With the presence of this spiritual pain, I don't believe that physical pain would be felt, little or much, even if the body were cut in pieces.

You will tell me that this feeling is an imperfection and ask why the soul doesn't conform to the will of God since it is so surrendered to him. Until now it could do this, and has spent its life doing so. As for now, the reasoning faculty is in such a condition that the soul is not the master of it, nor can the soul think of anything else than of why it is grieving, of how it is absent from its Good, and of why it should want to live. It feels a strange solitude, because no creature in all the earth provides it company, nor do I believe would any heavenly creature, not being the One whom it loves; rather, everything torments it. But the soul sees that it is like a person hanging, who cannot support himself on any earthly thing; nor can it ascend to heaven. On fire with this thirst, it cannot get to the water; and the thirst is not one that is endurable, but already at such a point that nothing will take it away. Nor does the soul desire that the thirst be taken away save by that water of which our Lord spoke to the Samaritan woman [John 4:7–15]. Yet no one gives such water to the soul.

O God, help me! Lord, how you afflict your lovers! But everything is small in comparison with what you give them afterward. It's natural that what is worth much costs much. Moreover, if the suffering is to purify this soul so that it might enter the seventh dwelling place—just as those who will enter heaven must be cleansed in purgatory—it is as small as a drop of water in the sea. Furthermore, in spite of all this torment and affliction, which cannot be surpassed, I believe, by any earthly afflictions (for this person had suffered many bodily as well as spiritual pains, but they all seemed nothing in comparison with this suffering), the soul feels that the pain is precious; so precious—it understands very well—that one could not deserve it. However, this awareness is not of a kind that alleviates the suffering in any way. But with this knowledge, the soul suffers the pain very willingly and would suffer it all its life, if God were to be thereby served; although the soul would not then die once, but be always dying, for truly the suffering is no less than death.

Well, let us consider, sisters, those who are in hell, who do not have this conformity or this consolation and spiritual delight that is placed by God in the soul; nor do they see that their suffering is beneficial, but they always suffer more and more. The torments of the soul are so much more severe than those of the body, and the torment souls in hell suffer is incomparably greater than the suffering we have here mentioned, and must, it is seen, last forever and ever. What, then, will the suffering of these unfortunate souls be? And what can we do or suffer in so short a life that would amount to anything if we were thereby to free ourselves of those terrible and eternal torments? I tell you it would be impossible to explain how keenly felt is the suffering of the soul, and how different it is from that of the body, if one had not experienced these things. And the Lord himself desires that we understand this, so that we may know the extraordinary debt we owe him for bringing us to a state in which, through his mercy, we hope he will free us and pardon our sins.

Well, to return to what we were dealing with—for we left this soul with much pain—this pain lasts only a short while in such intensity. At the most it will last three or four hours, in my opinion, because if it were to last a long while, natural weakness would not be able to endure it unless by a miracle. It has happened that the experience lasted no more than a quarter of an hour, but left the soul in pieces. Truly, that time the person lost her senses completely, and the pain came in its rigor merely from her hearing a word about life's not ending. This happened while she was engaged in conversation during Easter week, the last day of the octave, after she had spent all of Easter in so much dryness she almost didn't know it was Easter. In no way can the soul resist. It can no more do so than it can, if thrown in a fire, stop flames from having heat and burning it. This feeling is not one that can be concealed from others, but those who are present are aware of the great danger in which the person lies, although they cannot be witnesses to what is taking place interiorly. True, they provide some company, as though they were shadows; and so, like shadows, do all earthly things appear to that person.

And that you realize, in case you might sometime have this experience, what is due to our weakness, it happens at times that while in that state, as you have seen, the soul dies with the desire to die. For the fire afflicts so much that seemingly hardly anything keeps the soul from leaving the body. The soul truly fears and, lest it end up dying, would want the pain to abate. The soul indeed understands that this fear is from natural weakness, because on the other hand its desire to die is not taken away. Nor can a remedy be found to remove this pain until the Lord himself takes it away, usually by means of a great rapture, or with some vision, where the true Comforter consoles and strengthens the soul that it might desire to live as long as God wills.

This experience is a painful one, but the soul is left with the most beneficial effects, and fear of the trials that can come its way is lost. When compared to the painful feeling experienced in the soul, the trials don't seem to amount to anything. The benefits are such that one would be pleased to suffer the pain often. But one can in no way do this, nor is there any means for suffering the experience again. The soul must wait until the Lord desires to give this favor, just as there is no way to resist it or remove it when it comes. The soul is left with greater contempt for the world than before, because it sees that nothing in the world was any help to it in that torment, and it is much more detached from creatures because it now sees that only the Creator can console and satisfy it. And it has greater fear of offending him, taking more care not to do so, because it sees that he can also torment as well as console.

Two experiences, it seems to me, that lie on this spiritual path put a person in danger of death. The one is this pain, for it truly is a danger, and no small one; the other is overwhelming joy and delight, which reaches so extraordinary a peak that, indeed, the soul, I think, swoons to the point that it is hardly kept from leaving the body— indeed, its happiness could not be considered small.

Here you will see, sisters, whether I was right in saying that courage is necessary, and whether when you ask the Lord for these favors he is right in answering as he did the sons of Zebedee, "Are you able to drink the chalice?" [Matt. 20:22].

I believe all of us, sisters, will answer yes; and very rightly so, for His Majesty gives strength to the one he sees has need of it. He defends these souls in all things; when they are persecuted and criticized, he answers for them as he did for the Magdalene [Luke 7:40–48]—if not through words, through deeds. And in the very end, before they die, he will pay for everything at once, as you will now see. May he be blessed forever, and may all creatures praise him, amen.

THE SEVENTH
DWELLING PLACES

Chapter 2

Explains the difference between spiritual
union and spiritual marriage. Describes
this difference through some delicate
comparisons.

Now then, let us deal with the divine and spiritual marriage, although this great favor does not come to its perfect fullness as long as we live; for if we were to withdraw from God, this remarkable blessing would be lost.

The first time the favor is granted, His Majesty desires to show himself to the soul through an imaginative vision of his most sacred humanity, so that the soul will understand and not be ignorant of receiving this sovereign gift; with other persons the favor will be received in another form. With regard to the one of whom we are speaking, the Lord represented himself to her, just after she had received Communion, in the form of shining splendor, beauty, and majesty, as he was after his resurrection, and told her that now it was time that she consider as her own what belonged to him and that he would take care of what was hers, and he spoke other words destined more to be heard than to be mentioned.

It may seem that this experience was nothing new, since at other times the Lord had represented himself to the soul in such a way. The experience was so different that it left her indeed stupefied and frightened: first, because this vision came with great force; second, because of the words the Lord spoke to her and also because in the interior of her soul, where he represented himself to her, she had not seen other visions except the former one. You must understand that there is the greatest difference between all the previous visions and those of this dwelling place. Between the spiritual betrothal and the spiritual marriage the difference is as great as that which exists between two who are betrothed and between two who can no longer be separated.

I have already said that even though these comparisons are used, because there are no others better suited to our purpose, it should be understood that in this state there is no more thought of the body than if the soul were not in it, but one's thought is only of the spirit. In the spiritual marriage, there is still much less remembrance of the body, because this secret union takes place in the very interior center of the soul, which must be where God himself is, and in my opinion there is no need of any door for him to enter. I say there is no need of any door because everything that has been said up until now seems to take place by means of the senses and faculties, and this appearance of the humanity of the Lord must also. But that which comes to pass in the union of the spiritual marriage is very different. The Lord appears in this center of the soul not in an imaginative vision, but in an intellectual one, although more delicate than those mentioned, as he appeared to the apostles without entering through the door when he said to them *pax vobis* [John 20:19–21]. What God communicates here to the soul in an instant is a secret so great and a favor so sublime—and the delight the soul experiences so extreme—that I don't know what to compare it to. I can say only that the Lord wishes to reveal for that moment, in a more sublime manner than through any spiritual vision or taste, the glory of heaven. One can say no more—insofar as can be understood—than that the soul, I mean, the spirit, is made one with God. For since His Majesty is also spirit, he has wished to show his love for us by giving some persons understanding of the point to which this love reaches, so that we might praise his grandeur. For he has desired to be so joined with the creature that, just as those who are married cannot be separated, he doesn't want to be separated from the soul.

The spiritual betrothal is different, for the two often separate. And the union is also different because, even though it is the joining of two things into one, in the end the two can be separated and each remains by itself. We observe this ordinarily, for the favor of union with the Lord passes quickly, and afterward the soul remains without that company; I mean, without awareness of it. In this other favor from the Lord, no. The soul always remains with its God in that center. Let us say that the union is like the joining of two wax candles to such an extent that the flame coming from them is but one, or that the wick, the flame, and the wax are all one. But afterward one candle can be easily separated from the other and there are two candles; the same holds for the wick. In the spiritual marriage the union is like what we have when rain falls from the sky into a river or fount; all is water, for the rain that fell from heaven cannot be divided or separated from the water of the river. Or it is like what we have when a little stream enters the sea; there is no means of separating the two. Or like the bright light entering a room through two different windows; although the streams of light are separate when entering the room, they become one.

Perhaps this is what St. Paul means in saying, "He that is joined or united to the Lord becomes one spirit with him" [1 Cor. 6:17], and is referring to this sovereign marriage, presupposing that His Majesty has brought the soul to it through union. And he also says, "For me to live is Christ, and to die is gain" [Phil. 1:21]. The soul as well, I think, can say these words now, because this state is the place where the little butterfly we mentioned dies, and with the greatest joy because its life is now Christ.

And that its life is Christ is understood better, with the passing of time, by the effects this life has. Through some secret aspirations the soul understands clearly that it is God who gives life to our soul. These aspirations come very, very often in such a living way that they can in no way be doubted. The soul feels them very clearly, even though they are indescribable. But the feeling is so powerful that sometimes the soul cannot avoid the loving expressions they cause, such as: O Life of my life! Sustenance that sustains me! and things of this sort. For from those divine breasts where it seems God is always sustaining the soul there flow streams of milk bringing comfort to all the people of the castle. It seems the Lord desires that in some manner these others in the castle may enjoy the great deal the soul is enjoying and that from that full-flowing river, where this tiny fount is swallowed up, a spurt of that water will sometimes be directed toward the sustenance of those who in corporeal things must serve these two who are wed. Just as a distracted person would feel this water if he were suddenly bathed in it, and would be unable to avoid feeling it, so are these operations recognized, and even with greater certitude. For just as a great gush of water could not reach us if it didn't have a source, as I have said, so it is understood clearly that there is Someone in the interior depths who shoots these arrows and gives life to this life, and that there is a Sun in the interior of the soul from which a brilliant light proceeds and is sent to the faculties. The soul, as I have said, does not move from that center nor is its peace lost; for the very One who gave peace to the apostles when they were together can give it to the soul.

It has occurred to me that this greeting of the Lord must have amounted to much more than is apparent from its sound, as well as our Lord's words to the glorious Magdalene that she go in peace [Luke 7:50]. Since the Lord's words are effected in us as deeds, they must have worked in those souls already disposed in such a manner that everything corporeal in them was taken away and they were left in pure spirit. Thus the soul could be joined in this heavenly union with the uncreated spirit. For it is very certain that in emptying ourselves of all that is creature and detaching ourselves from it for the love of God, the same Lord will fill us with himself. And thus, while Jesus our Lord was once praying for his apostles—I don't remember where—he said that they were one with the Father and with him, just as Jesus Christ our Lord is in the Father and the Father is in him [John 17:21]. I don't know what greater love there can be than this. And all of us are included here, for His Majesty said, "I ask not only for them, but for all those who also will believe in me"; and he says, "I am in them" [John 17:20, 23].

O God help me, how true these words are! And how well they are understood by the soul who is in this prayer and sees for itself. How well we would all understand them, if it were not for our own fault, since the words of Jesus Christ, our King and Lord, cannot fail. But since we fail by not disposing ourselves and turning away from all that can hinder this light, we do not see ourselves in this mirror that we contemplate, where our image is engraved.

Well, to return to what we were saying. The Lord puts the soul in this dwelling of his, which is the center of the soul itself. They say that the empyreal heaven, where the Lord is, does not move as do the other heavens; similarly, it seems, in the soul that enters here there are none of those movements that usually take place in the faculties and the imagination and do harm to the soul, nor do these stirrings take away its peace.

It seems I'm saying that when the soul reaches this state in which God grants it this favor, it is sure of its salvation and safe from falling again. I do not say such a thing, and wherever I so speak that it seems the soul is secure, this should be taken to mean as long as the divine Majesty keeps it in his hand and it does not offend him. At least I know certainly that the soul doesn't consider itself safe, even though it sees itself in this state and the state has lasted for some years. But it goes about with much greater fear than before, guarding itself from any small offense against God and with the strongest desire to serve him, as will be said farther on, and with habitual pain and confusion at seeing the little it can do and the great deal to which it is obliged. This pain is no small cross, but a very great penance. For when this soul does penance, the delight will be greater in the measure that the penance is greater. The true penance comes when God takes away the soul's health and strength for doing penance. Even though I have mentioned elsewhere the great pain this lack causes, the pain is much more intense here. All these things must come to the soul from its roots, from where it is planted. The tree that is beside the running water is fresher and gives more fruit. What is there, then, to marvel at in the desires this soul has, since its true spirit has become one with the heavenly water we mentioned?

Now then, to return to what I was saying, it should not be thought that the faculties, senses, and passions are always in this peace; the soul is, yes. But in those other dwelling places, times of war, trial, and fatigue are never lacking; however, they are such that they do not take the soul from its place and its peace, that is, as a rule.

This center of our soul, or this spirit, is something so difficult to explain, and even believe in, that I think, sisters, I'll not give you the temptation to disbelieve what I say, for I do not know how to explain this center. That there are trials and sufferings and that at the same time the soul is in peace is a difficult thing to explain. I want to make one or more comparisons for you. Please God, I may be saying something through them; but if not, I know that I'm speaking the truth in what I say.

The King is in his palace, and there are many wars in his kingdom and many painful things going on, but not on that account does he fail to be at his post. So here, even though in those other dwelling places there is much tumult and there are many poisonous creatures and the noise is heard, no one enters that center dwelling place and makes the soul leave. Nor do the things the soul hears make it leave; even though they cause it some pain, the suffering is not such as to disturb it and take away its peace. The passions are now conquered and have a fear of entering the center, because they would go away from there more subdued.

Our entire body may ache; but if the head is sound, the head will not ache just because the body aches.

I am laughing to myself over these comparisons, for they do not satisfy me, but I don't know any others. You may think what you want; what I have said is true.

Chapter 4

Concludes by explaining what she thinks our Lord's purpose is in granting such great favors to the soul and how it is necessary that Martha and Mary join together. This chapter is very beneficial.

You must not think, sisters, that the effects I mentioned are always present in these souls. Hence, where I remember, I say "ordinarily." For sometimes our Lord leaves these individuals in

their natural state, and then it seems that all the poisonous creatures from the outskirts and other dwelling places of this castle
band together to take revenge for the time they were unable to
have these souls under their control.

True, this natural state lasts only a short while, a day at most or
a little more. And in this great disturbance, usually occasioned by
some event, the soul's gain through the good company it is in
becomes manifest. For the Lord gives the soul great stability and
good resolutions not to deviate from his service in anything. But
it seems this determination increases, and these souls do not
deviate through even a very slight first movement. As I say, this
disturbance is rare, but our Lord does not want the soul to forget
its being, so that, for one thing, it might always be humble; for
another, that it might better understand the tremendous favor it
receives, what it owes His Majesty, and that it might praise him.

Nor should it pass through your minds that, since these souls
have such determination and strong desires not to commit any
imperfection for anything on earth, they fail to commit many
imperfections, and even sins. Advertently, no; for the Lord must
give souls such as these very particular help against such a thing. I
mean venial sins, for from what these souls can understand they
are free from mortal sins, although not immune. That they might
have some sins they don't know about is no small torment to
them. They also suffer torment in seeing souls go astray. Even
though in some way they have great hope that they themselves
will not be among these souls, they cannot help but fear when
they recall some of those persons Scripture mentions who, it

seems, were favored by the Lord, like Solomon, who communed so much with His Majesty, as I have said [1 Kings 11]. The one among you who feels safest should fear more, for "Blessed is the man who fears the Lord," says David [Ps. 112:1]. May His Majesty protect us always. To beseech him that we not offend him is the greatest security we can have. May he be praised forever, amen.

It will be good, sisters, to tell you the reason the Lord grants so many favors in this world. Although, if you have paid attention, you will have understood this in learning of their effects, I want to tell you again here, lest someone think that the reason is solely for the sake of giving delight to these souls; that thought would be a serious error. His Majesty couldn't grant us a greater favor than to give us a life that would be an imitation of the life his beloved Son lived. Thus I hold for certain that these favors are meant to fortify our weakness, as I have said here at times, that we may be able to imitate him in his great sufferings.

We have always seen that those who were closest to Christ our Lord were those with the greatest trials. Let us look at what his glorious Mother suffered and the glorious apostles. How do you think St. Paul could have suffered such very great trials? Through him we can see the effects visions and contemplation produce when from our Lord, and not from the imagination or the devil's deceit. Did St. Paul by chance hide himself in the enjoyment of these delights and not engage in anything else? You already see that he didn't have a day of rest, from what we can understand, and neither did he have any rest at night, since it was then that he earned his livelihood [1 Thess. 2:9]. I like very much the account about St. Peter's fleeing from prison and how our Lord appeared to him and told him, "I am on my way to Rome to be crucified again." We never recite the office of this feast, where this account is, that I don't find particular consolation. How did this favor from the Lord impress St. Peter or what did he do? He went straight to his death. And it was no small mercy from the Lord that Peter found someone to provide him with death.

O my sisters! How forgetful this soul, in which the Lord dwells in so particular a way, should be of its own rest, how little it should care for its honor, and how far it should be from wanting esteem in anything! For if it is with him very much, as is right, it should think little about itself. All its concern is taken up with how to please him more and how or where it will show him the love it bears him. This is the reason for prayer, my daughters, the purpose of this spiritual marriage: the birth always of good works, good works.

This is the true sign of a thing, or favor, being from God, as I have already told you. It benefits me little to be alone making acts of devotion to our Lord, proposing and promising to do wonders in his service, if I then go away and, when the occasion offers itself, do everything the opposite. I was wrong in saying it profits little, for everything having to do with God profits a great deal. And even though we are weak and do not carry out these resolutions afterward, sometimes His Majesty will give us the power to do so, even though, perhaps, doing so is burdensome to us, as is often true. Since he sees that a soul is very fainthearted, he gives it a severe trial, truly against its will, and brings this soul out of the trial with profit. Afterward, since the soul understands this, the fear lessens and one can offer oneself more willingly to him. I meant "it benefits me little" in comparison with how much greater the benefit is when our deeds conform with what we say in prayer; what cannot be done all at once can be done little by little. Let the soul bend its will if it wishes that prayer be beneficial to it, for within the corners of these little monasteries there will not be lacking many occasions for you to do so.

Keep in mind that I could not exaggerate the importance of this. Fix your eyes on the Crucified and everything will become small for you. If His Majesty showed us his love by means of such works and frightful torments, how is it that you want to please him only with words? Do you know what it means to be truly spiritual? It means becoming the slaves of God. Marked with his brand, which is that of the cross, spiritual persons, because now they have given him their liberty, can be sold by him as slaves of everyone, as he was. He doesn't thereby do them any harm or grant them a small favor. And if souls aren't determined about becoming his slave, let them be convinced that they are not making much progress, for this whole building, as I have said, has humility as its foundation. If humility is not genuinely present, for your own sake the Lord will not construct a high building, lest that building fall to the ground. Thus, sisters, that you might build on good foundations, strive to be the least and the slaves of all, looking at how or where you can please and serve them. What you do in this matter you do more for yourself than for them and lay stones so firmly that the castle will not fall.

I repeat, it is necessary that your foundation consist of more than prayer and contemplation. If you do not strive for the virtues and practice them, you will always be dwarfs. And, please God, it will be only a matter of not growing, for you already know that whoever does not increase decreases. I hold that love, where present, cannot possibly be content with remaining always the same.

It will seem to you that I am speaking with those who are beginning and that after this beginner's stage souls can rest. I have already told you that the calm these souls have interiorly is for the sake of their having much less calm exteriorly and much less desire to have exterior calm. What, do you think, is the reason for those inspirations (or to put it better, aspirations) I mentioned, and those messages the soul sends from the interior center to the people at the top of the castle and to the dwelling places outside the center where it is? Is it so that those outside might fall asleep? No, absolutely not! That the faculties, senses, and all that which is corporeal will not be idle, the soul wages more war from the center than it did when it was outside suffering with them, for then it didn't understand the tremendous gain trials bring. Perhaps they were the means by which God brought it to the center, and the company it has gives it much greater strength than ever. For if here below, as David says, in the company of the saints we will become saints [Ps. 18:26], there is no reason to doubt that, being united with the Strong One through so sovereign a union of spirit with spirit, fortitude will cling to such a soul; and so we shall understand what fortitude the saints had for suffering and dying.

It is very certain that from that fortitude which clings to it there the soul assists all those who are in the castle, and even the body itself, which often, seemingly, does not feel the strength. But the soul is fortified by the strength it has from drinking wine in this wine cellar, where its Spouse has brought it [Song of Sol. 2:4] and from where he doesn't allow it to leave; and strength flows back to the weak body, just as food placed in the stomach strengthens the head and the whole body. Thus the soul has its share of misfortune while it lives. However much it does, the interior strength increases and thus, too, the war that is waged; for everything seems like a trifle to it. The great penances that many saints—especially the glorious Magdalene, who had always been surrounded by so much luxury—performed must have come from this center; also that hunger which our Father Elijah had for the honor of his God [1 Kings 19:10] and which St. Dominic and St. Francis had so as to draw souls to praise God. I tell you, though they were forgetful of themselves, their suffering must have been great.

This is what I want us to strive for, my sisters; and let us desire and be occupied in prayer not for the sake of our enjoyment, but so as to have this strength to serve. Let's refuse to take an unfamiliar path, for we shall get lost at the most opportune time. It would indeed be novel to think of having these favors from God through a path other than the one he took and the one followed by all his saints. May the thought never enter our minds. Believe me, Martha and Mary must join together in order to show hospitality to the Lord and have him always present and not host him badly by failing to give him something to eat. How would Mary, always seated at his feet, provide him with food if her sister did not help her? [Luke 10:38–42]. His food is that in every way possible we draw souls that they may be saved and praise him always.

You will make two objections: one, that he said that Mary had chosen the better part. The answer is that she had already performed the task of Martha, pleasing the Lord by washing his feet and drying them with her hair [Luke 7:38–39]. Do you think it would be a small mortification for a woman of nobility like her to wander through these streets (and perhaps alone, because her fervent love made her unaware of what she was doing) and enter a house she had never entered before and afterward suffer the criticism of the Pharisee and the very many other things she must have suffered? The people saw a woman like her change so much—and, as we know, she was among such malicious people—and they saw her friendship with the Lord, whom they vehemently abhorred, and that she wanted to become a saint, since obviously she would have changed her manner of dress and everything else. All of that was enough to cause them to comment on the life she had formerly lived. If nowadays there is so much gossip against persons who are not so notorious, what would have been said then? I tell you, sisters, the better part came after many trials and much mortification, for even if there were no other trial than to see His Majesty abhorred, that would be an intolerable one. Moreover, the many trials that afterward she suffered at the death of the Lord and in the years that she subsequently lived in his absence must have been a terrible torment.

You see she wasn't always in the delight of contemplation at the feet of the Lord.

The other objection you will make is that you are unable to bring souls to God, that you do not have the means; that you would do it willingly but that, not being teachers or preachers as were the apostles, you do not know how. This objection I have answered at times in writing, but I don't know if I did so in this *Castle*. Yet since the matter is something I believe is passing through your mind on account of the desires God gives you, I will not fail to respond here. I already told you elsewhere that sometimes the devil gives us great desires, so that we will avoid setting ourselves to the task at hand, serving our Lord in possible things, and instead be content with having desired the impossible. Apart from the fact that by prayer you will be helping greatly, you need not be desiring to benefit the whole world, but must concentrate on those who are in your company, and thus your deed will be greater since you are more obliged toward them. Do you think such deep humility, your mortification, service of all and great charity toward them, and love of the Lord are of little benefit? This fire of love in you enkindles their souls, and with every other virtue you will be always awakening them. Such service will not be small, but very great and very pleasing to the Lord. By what you do in deed—that which you can—His Majesty will understand that you would do much more. Thus he will give you the reward he would if you had gained many souls for him.

You will say that such service does not convert souls, because all the sisters you deal with are already good. Who has appointed you judge in this matter? The better they are, the more pleasing their praises will be to our Lord, and the more their prayer will profit their neighbor.

In sum, my sisters, what I conclude with is that we shouldn't build castles in the air. The Lord doesn't look so much at the greatness of our works as at the love with which they are done. And if we do what we can, His Majesty will enable us each day to do more and more, provided that we do not quickly tire. But during the little while this life lasts—and perhaps it will last a shorter time than each one thinks—let us offer the Lord interiorly and exteriorly the sacrifice we can. His Majesty will join it with that which he offered on the cross to the Father for us. Thus even though our works are small, they will have the value our love for him would have merited had they been great.

May it please His Majesty, my sisters and daughters, that we all reach that place where we may ever praise him. Through the merits of his Son who lives and reigns forever and ever, may he give me the grace to carry out something of what I tell you, amen. For I tell you that my confusion is great, and thus I ask you through the same Lord that in your prayers you do not forget this poor wretch.

EPILOGUE

Although when I began writing this book I am sending you I did so with the aversion I mentioned in the beginning, now that I am finished I admit the work has brought me much happiness, and I consider the labor, though I confess it was small, well spent. Considering the strict enclosure and the few things you have for your entertainment, my sisters, and that your buildings are not always as large as would be fitting for your monasteries, I think it will be a consolation for you to delight in this interior castle, since without permission from the prioress you can enter and take a walk through it at any time.

True, you will not be able to enter all the dwelling places through your own efforts, even though these efforts may seem to you great, unless the Lord of the castle himself brings you there. Hence I advise you to use no force if you meet with any resistance, for you will thereby anger him in such a way that he will never allow you to enter them. He is very fond of humility. By considering that you do not deserve even to enter the third, you will more quickly win the favor to reach the fifth. And you will be able to serve him from there in such a way, continuing to walk through them often, that he will bring you into the very dwelling place he has for himself. You need never leave this latter dwelling place unless called by the prioress, whose will this great Lord desires that you comply with as much as if it were his own. Even though you are frequently outside through her command, you will always find the door open when you return. Once you get used to enjoying this castle, you will find rest in all things, even those involving much labor, for you will have the hope of returning to the castle, which no one can take from you.

Although no more than seven dwelling places were discussed, in each of these there are many others, below and above and to the sides, with lovely gardens and fountains and labyrinths, such delightful things that you would want to be dissolved in praises of the great God who created the soul in his own image and likeness. If you find something good in the way I have explained this to you, believe that indeed His Majesty said it so as to make you happy; the bad that you might find is said by me.

Through the strong desire I have to play some part in helping you serve my God and Lord, I ask that each time you read this work you, in my name, praise His Majesty fervently and ask for the increase of his church and for light for the Lutherans. As for me, ask him to pardon my sins and deliver me from purgatory, for perhaps by the mercy of God I will be there when this is given you to read—if it may be seen by you after having been examined by learned men. If anything is erroneous, it is so because I didn't know otherwise; and I submit in everything to what the holy Roman Catholic Church holds, for in this church I live, declare my faith, and promise to live and die.

May God our Lord be forever praised and blessed, amen, amen.

This writing was finished in the monastery of St. Joseph of Avila in the year 1577, the eve before the feast of St. Andrew, for the glory of God, who lives and reigns forever and ever, amen.

ABOUT THE EDITOR

HarperCollins Spiritual Classics Series Editor Emilie Griffin has long been interested in the classics of the devotional life. She has written a number of books on spiritual formation and transformation, including *Clinging: The Experience of Prayer* and *Wilderness Time: A Guide to Spiritual Retreat*. With Richard J. Foster she coedited *Spiritual Classics: Selected Readings on the Twelve Spiritual Disciplines*. Her latest book is *Wonderful and Dark Is this Road: Discovering the Mystic Path*. She is a board member of Renovaré and leads retreats and workshops throughout the United States. She and her husband, William, live in Alexandria, Louisiana.

THE CLASSICS OF **WESTERN SPIRITUALITY**
A LIBRARY OF THE GREAT SPIRITUAL MASTERS

These volumes contain original writings of universally acknowledged teachers within the Catholic, Protestant, Eastern Orthodox, Jewish, Islamic, and American Indian traditions.

The Classics of Western Spirituality unquestionably provide the most in-depth, comprehensive, and accessible panorama of Western mysticism ever attempted. From the outset, the Classics has insisted on the highest standards for these volumes, including new translations from the original languages, and helpful introductions and other aids by internationally recognized scholars and religious thinkers, designed to help the modern reader to come to a better appreciation of these works that have nourished the three monotheistic faiths for centuries.

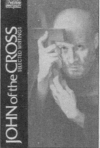

The Cloud of Unknowing
Edited and Introduced
by James Walsh
0-8091-2332-0 $22.95

Teresa of Avila
Edited and Introduced
by Kieran Kavanaugh, O.C.D.
0-8091-2254-5 $22.95

John of the Cross
Edited and Introduced
by Kieran Kavanaugh, O.C.D.
0-8091-2839-X $21.95

John and Charles Wesley
Edited and Introduced
by Frank Whaling
0-8091-2368-1 $26.95

For more information on the
CLASSICS OF WESTERN SPIRITUALITY, contact Paulist Press
(800) 218-1903 • **www.paulistpress.com**